THE
ANSWER

THE
ANSWER

42 Days of connecting with your
Authentic Personal Power

Iesha Delune

BALBOA.
PRESS
A DIVISION OF HAY HOUSE

Balboa Press books may be ordered through booksellers or by contacting:

Balboa Press
A Division of Hay House
1663 Liberty Drive
Bloomington, IN 47403
www.balboapress.com.au
1-(877) 407-4847

ISBN: 978-1-4525-1118-4 (sc)
ISBN: 978-1-4525-1119-1 (e)

Printed in the United States of America

Balboa Press rev. date: 08/27/2013

Contents

Acknowledgements

There are many people I wish to thank for the abundant and varied ways I have been inspired to create this book and supported in its completion.

Most importantly I want to thank every client and student that I have had the honour and pleasure of working with—without your honesty, bravery, and desire to be authentically, personally powerful this book would never have come into being.

I wish to thank my beautiful children. I love and appreciate you so much for keeping me smiling and challenged in continual learning with boundaries, communication and life balance. From pregnancy you've been my inspiration to completely prioritise being the best 'me' that I can be. Without you I might still be sitting behind a desk in a *blurk*y job, dreaming this dream I am now living—working in a way that makes my heart sing.

Thank you to my sister and parents for the incalculable hours of support you lovingly provided as I began my business and importantly for celebrating its growth with me. Also, for being so proud of my successes even before they were evident.

Thank you from the depths of my being to the following people who simply must be named: Mel McMaster for being such an awesome *blurk*-eliminator in my life; Chris Callister for our weekly tune-up and reminder that everything is going to be OK; Kez Ellis for making sure that I got out and danced and sang and had a ball even though I was busy with book-writing, business owning, and all of life's other necessities (and for being the first reader of my manuscript with all the positive encouragement and practical support that followed); Rosie Brown for role-modelling that this book publishing thing can be done and for the *destuckification* when required; Martha Dais for telling me that I really needed to share my wisdom with the world; Jodi Switzer for believing in me and always encouraging me to take action towards my goals; Andrew Griffiths for the 'central question' concept that had me ditch my first 26,000 words and start again (producing a much better book!); Issam Kadamani—for so many of the transformative tools I use daily (for myself and others) I learned from your beautiful self; Nick Rose for nailing it with the title; Stacey Dobis for her support, enthusiasm, and encouragement for this project and likewise to Joc Hansen and James Tsakalos.

Thank you to you all!

Introduction

Welcome! You're ace and here's what it's all about

Hello and welcome to *The Answer*, a journey of self-discovery to assist you in connecting with your Authentic Personal Power.

The next 42 days will be an exploration into, around and through your innate resources of mind, body and energy. This is your equipment for life, and you'll finish this book understanding yourself more deeply and knowing that you are a powerful being indeed.

This is a practical book that teaches you about how your brain, body and energy work together to create your life experiences. Throughout the book, you will be evaluating where you are now and how successfully you've been using these resources. You will learn how to run your brain, body, and energy together for the purpose of never, EVER, feeling like you're not in charge of your life and circumstances again.

This is an instructive and useful manual providing you with information and exercises to equip you with tools to practically use in your daily life.

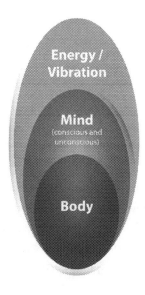

Your brain, body and life-force energy are inseparably working together to create your every experience and 'state of being' from depression to exhilaration. In this book, you'll be guided through each of these areas and will gain a deep understanding that you can work on any one area to uplift the others. There is a difference between a 'state of mind' and a 'state of being'. In this book, I use the latter because 'being' is mental, physical and energetic. When I am using the word 'wholistic' it is these elements of mind, body and energy that I am referring to.

Think about the last time you felt extremely angry. Remember how your body felt, what your posture was like, what your energy was like and what was running through your head. It might have been a tight chest, scrunched face, aggressive thoughts and an energetic fire in your belly to take some action. You might have been making pictures in your mind of other times you've been angry or how satisfying it would be to take that action you imagined.

Think about the last time you felt genuinely excited about something. Remember how your body felt, what your energy level was like and what was running through your head. You might have had a buzzy feeling in your chest and stomach, a huge smile on your face that sparkled in your eyes and experienced an uplifted, light energy. You might have been making pictures in your head of the other times you've done this exciting thing or what it will be like when you do whatever it is that you're excited about.

There truly isn't an experience that's just mental or just physical or just an energetic occurrence. That's why here you'll be learning to utilise them all.

There are so many books in the self-development genre that teach about state of mind and changing your thoughts to positive ones. Personally, I've found many of them particularly useful, but I've also found gaps that I wanted to fill with this book.

Firstly, there are certain intense emotional states where changing your thoughts is damned-near impossible! So I wanted to provide a range of things you can do without always tackling your brain head-on.

Secondly, there are intense emotional circumstances where you get quite stuck in your *blurk* (that heavy, dark, unmotivated place) and can't seem to shift out of it any way you try. This can sometimes take days to wear off and in some cases a *lot* longer. It *always* gets in the way of life being enjoyable and you feeling powerful, except for powerfully awful!. In this book, you'll learn that there is sometimes an unconscious benefit to staying in that *blurk*. Your unconscious mind is designed to keep your body safe, and functioning and sometimes that *blurk* is there for a very important reason. In those cases, a new way of communicating with yourself is necessary, and you'll be learning how to do just that.

Thirdly, I wanted to make it a bite-size experience and offer a structure in which there is something to learn and assimilate each day. It's too easy to read a self-help book over a couple of days and then not apply any of the new information in your daily experience.

My aims:

- Thoroughly explain how you are practically and wholistically creating your life experiences. It's not spiritual woo-woo; you actually do create the life you have and that means you can create changes too!
- To leave you knowing that you are totally in charge of your life and circumstances.
- To provide you with a huge list of practical tools for uplifting your 'now' (which will directly result in an uplifted future).
- And hopefully make you laugh at least a few times.

My ultimate intention is for you to know that you have the absolute power to change anything you wish to. Your life is like a horse and cart ride; you are the driver, you have the reins, and you get to choose the cart and horse too.

What you, the reader, can do to get the most out of this book:

1) **Read each day with an open mind.** The moment we decide, "Oh. I already know this." We switch off the learning process. Remaining open, means a willingness to learn and experience and it's a wonderful state to be in as often as you can be in life.
2) **Do all of the exercises contained within.** Whether this is the first or the fiftieth (or 150th) personal development book you've read, completing the exercises is an extremely important part of achieving the results you wanted to experience when you chose to start reading.
3) **Take it one day at a time.** If you are truly struggling with one of the days, then take it as slow as you need to. There are no prizes handed out for whomever whizzes through the text the fastest, so give yourself permission for it to take as long as it takes.

For most of us, feeling confident means knowing what you are doing. By the end of this book, you'll know and will have experienced how your equipment-for-life works. You won't have to wait around hoping that ace stuff starts to happen. You can be in your amazing, and renewed body interacting with the world around you in a whole new way and making it happen.

I've written this book with respect and love for my fellow human beings. I have personally experienced the heart-braking pain of being disconnected from my personal power and completely unaware of my resources. I've lived in the relationships one chooses when they loathe themselves, and I've treated my body with the disrespect that matched my self-esteem. It took a lot of years to claw my way back up and out of living that way. I read a lot of books, tried a lot of different therapies and went to a lot of workshops. As time went on and I started to feel better, I engaged in the dream that I would help other people who felt the way that I did before I began my journey into the strong sense of self-worth and personal power that is now my life. I invested into practitioner training with modalities that had created the greatest improvements. I've ended up with a diverse range of highly effective skills that I bring to the business I began in 2004, Wholistic Vitality.

I've seen that state of disconnection in thousands of one-on-one sessions and in the classes I have run now for nearly a decade. I've had the honour and absolute pleasure of watching that disconnection be positively transformed with the information and tools I'll be sharing with you in this book.

I have a heartfelt passion to encourage and support people to uncover their self-worth and connect with their confidence. I believe in every person's ability to learn, grow, love and be empowered by choosing to connect with all that they are.

So, thank you for being here and let the choices begin by choosing to experience Day 1 . . .

Cause and Effect Part 1

The framework for real-life empowerment

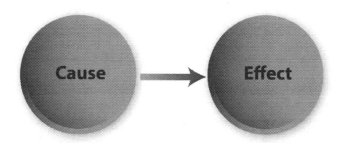

You have probably heard the terms *cause* and *effect* throughout your life and there are many ways in which to make sense of them. It's part of what we are taught growing up. If you do this thing, that thing will happen. If you don't tie your shoelaces properly, you could trip and break your arm. If you studied science at school you might have heard that cause-and-effect is Newton's third law, for every action there is a reaction of the same intensity. In Buddhist Sanskrit, it is the law of Karma—as we sow, so shall we reap. Whichever way you choose to think about these words, right now the basic premise is this: things aren't happening by mere chance.

Since I began studying metaphysics in 1997, I have seen many people turn away from their spiritual path when confronted with this concept. They say: "So, I created the car accident I had, did I?" or "Are you saying, my mother created her cancer? This is bullshit!"

For now, I invite you to think of it more like this: Empowerment comes when we firstly acknowledge that we have the ability to make decisions and be a part of choosing our outcomes. I want to offer you the empowerment that comes from taking total responsibility for your own situation.

I'm not suggesting you necessarily leap on board with, "I-chose-everything-that's-ever-happened-in-my-life." I am suggesting that you have the definite experience of acknowledging when you are in either position, whether it be *cause* or *effect* in your life and then choosing which feels best.

Let me give you an example. Many years ago I worked with Pen, a single mother, who had a 50/50 custody arrangement with her ex-husband. She would have a week with her daughter and a week without her, and she was heartbroken about it. She was of the opinion that this horrible situation was out of her control, and there was no possible way she could feel anything other than hurt, anger and pain every time she had to say goodbye to her daughter. Before we started our work together, she couldn't see that she had total control over how she was responding to losing that time with her child. For her, the physical circumstances were a 'fact' and her mind wouldn't let her see past this point. She did not have legal grounds to contest the custody decision and she felt doomed to feeling this painful loss.

Throughout our work together, she released the stored up reservoir of pain, loss, hurt and anger from her 'system', much of which existed before her marriage separation. With healing and new unconscious strategies, Pen was able to generate new responses to her situation. She started attending regular yoga classes, changed her diet, and left her full-time job that she described as a "soulless means to an end." She began her own business and guess what . . . she ended up having MORE time with her daughter than previously. How? Well, Pen worked hard during the week her daughter was with her dad, and then, for the first time in her child's life, she was able to pick her up from school and not use any childcare or school care services. As her business established itself, she was even able to spend time with her daughter during the father's week, rather than her going into care until he finished work five days a week.

During her last session with me, Pen was telling me about the interstate holiday she'd just taken her daughter on which was also a first.

Pen took all that she'd learned, got into the *cause* side of the equation and made the most of her situation. She's now happier than ever before and having more fun experiences with her daughter and enjoying daily life more, too. The best part, she tells me, is feeling like such an awesome role model for her daughter as well!

It's extremely difficult to feel empowered and powerless all at the same time. If you are at the *effect* of an upsetting situation, it is very hard to see the choices available to you. This creates disempowerment. However, if you change your thinking back to being at *cause*, you can now feel empowered to choose how you respond. Thinking or feeling like you're at the *effect* of an outside person or situation creates disempowerment. Noticing that's how you are feeling and shifting into *cause* gives you an internal victory—you can now choose how to respond to this thing that is going on outside (or inside) of you.

Cause and effect give us fabulous feedback, too. It gives you permission to try things and see if it gets you the effect you're wanting. If not, try something else and see what effect that generates.

Let me make a very clear distinction here between *understanding cause and effect* and *everything's-your-fault*. These two things are actually extremely different!

I was working with a client who was feeling majorly unsupported in her relationship with her partner after the birth of their first child. She would experience surges of rage and then leap into her distorted version of the cause and effect principle and say things like this to herself: "I'm responsible for how I feel, not him; I should stop expecting anything from my husband, I chose him, this is just how he is; if I could just have no expectations then I wouldn't get so upset; it's my fault for having expectations; I should love him unconditionally without him having to do anything; I should just choose to be happy; if I choose to change my standards, could I be less angry?" . . . you get the idea. She would mentally try to justify the rage away by taking responsibility for it, but it was still wholly there in her body and just a hair trigger away.

As you become more and more aware of the cause and effect principle in your life, please know that while you are responsible for your life and your responses this DOES NOT MEAN that you need to tolerate or accept the behaviour of others when it is not OK for you.

You're responsible for what you allow to happen, and you're responsible for communicating how you feel about what's happened or is happening. It's unfair and usually unproductive to subject someone to bursts of unexpressed emotions such as blowing up over a wet towel on the floor, when actually you're feeling disrespected in a deep and fundamental way. How can you have a meaningful relationship if you don't allow your partner to know about the affect they have on you? If you have communicated the effects and they've said, "Take it or leave it honey, I ain't changing,"—well then you've still got choices and at least your relationship is authentic. In the example above, my client hadn't expressed anything, she was doing the, "Everything's OK honey," when she was actually contemplating whether their relationship could survive.

On Day 6, we will talk about Empowered Communication—How to own your stuff and still talk about how you feel. The tools shared in this section were very useful for this client and her husband. I'm happy to say they are still together and in a much stronger and more connected place than before.

Cause and effect is not a tool for disempowerment—it's a tool for empowerment! And it can change your life if you let it.

Today's Commitment to Authentic Personal Power

1) Answer these:

- Where do you feel in control (at *cause*)?

- Where do you feel like someone else has control and you have to live with the effects (at *effect*)?

- Do particular people in your life promote being in one position more than the other?

2) As you go about the next 24 hours, focus your attention on which position you're in—*cause* or *effect*.

It is very normal to oscillate between the two positions depending on what you're doing, whom you're with, and how you're feeling.

So, ask yourself: "Am I at *cause*? Am I noticing what is going on around me and enjoying the effects or noticing the feedback and choosing new causes? Or am I at *effect*?"

When you notice yourself at *effect*, what are you able to do about it?

Before going on to Day 2, take a moment to reflect on what you learned and what you noticed over the time you were practicing being aware of *cause* and *effect*.

- How often were you able to notice a difference between being at *cause* and *effect*?

- What did you do about the times you found yourself at *effect*?

- Did you notice any patterns to the situations?

- How great did you feel when you were able to turn it around?

DAY 2

Your Thoughts Generate Your Feelings

The roles of your conscious and unconscious mind
Creating awareness—the road to freedom

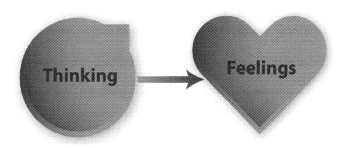

Your thoughts, right now, are generating how you're feeling, right now.

It's worth mentioning because sometimes, through sheer distraction from what's going on inside our minds, we can find ourselves in a feeling and think it just happened to us. It didn't. All of your feelings are made possible by what is going on inside your mind, and more deeply what you have inside you're unconscious mind in what I will be calling your *program*. Your *program* is the accumulation of every piece of data that's come through all of your senses since you were conceived and started growing your senses. It is my belief that we also contain information from our ancestors. As one example, in the physical sense, there are some lineages that process alcohol more efficiently due to the family tree's use of it for centuries. When I talk about your senses, I am referring to sight, hearing, touch, taste, smell and the other sense, which is interpreting the vibration around you. Whether you consider yourself particularly good at sensing energy or not, we are *all* exceptionally talented at it. Think about when you walk into an event like a rock concert, right before the headline act . . . the vibration is tangible as expectation and excitement. This has a very different energy to most funerals, even with the same number of people attending, whether you knew the person or not.

Even though I'm sure you may want to say, "Duh! I know this!" please stay with me. It really is always worth absolutely mastering the basics. I am sharing with you the building blocks for being at *cause*.

Think about one of the happiest moments of your life (and make it something there are no negative associations with e.g. the day I got my dream job . . . Oh yeah, and then my boss turned out to be a horrible, talentless chump). Choose a purely positive, happy memory from any point in your life, from your earliest memory to today.

If you can't think of a positive memory, I want you to make one up. Immerse yourself now into the future realisation of one of your goals or dreams. I want you to imagine yourself there; having reached this milestone . . . what's it like? How do you feel about yourself and your life? What are the sensations in your body? What thoughts are going on inside your head, and what can you hear going on around you? What do you look like to yourself and others? Go there now and experience the sensations.

Please make a mental note of what you see, hear, taste and smell. How do you feel, inside yourself as the imagining takes place?

Now think of a horrible memory. Choose a time that you felt guilty, hard-done-by, sad, frustrated, or one of those less enjoyable emotions. Really go there and do the same thing as above. How do you feel and what happens to your senses?

Please make a mental note of what you see, hear, taste and smell. How do you feel, inside yourself as the imagining takes place?

This exercise yields the most noticeable results when you choose extremely powerful memories, but regardless, I'm sure you noticed some key differences, yes? What happened to your face? What were the sensations in your body like? Buzzy? Sharp? Heavy? Dull? Moving or still? What happened with your breathing? Try it again with other memories if you didn't get a noticeable shift in your physiology.

Were you able to stay in the memory you chose or did other situations with similar feelings come up too?

You've probably heard, "Like attracts like," and this is particularly true emotionally. When you are experiencing a powerful emotion, it is extremely common to open the floodgates to all the other 'open' files of the same emotion. For example, when you're quite frustrated, it's very common to churn up lots of other, unresolved, frustrating experiences from your past. When you're experiencing heart-felt gratitude, it's very common to flash across other moments in life when you felt blessed and thankful. We are going to talk more about this in Day 19—The Frequency of Thoughts and Emotions. For now, just know that feelings will generally draw out of your unconscious *program* feelings of a similar nature because thinking pulls up files of the same kind of thinking. Have you ever noticed when you get a new kind of car that you suddenly see more of them than ever before on the road? Well this is kind of similar. Your unconscious mind goes, "Oh, I see that feeling frustrated/grateful is very important now, let me show you more of that."

In the spirit of being at *cause*, I want for you to know that there is no emotion that you can't move out of feeling by shifting your focus. Emotions do not come *at you* from the outside—they are generated by you from the inside. You cannot be "lost in love" or "in the grip of fear" or be "hit by wave after wave of remorse"—there is always a choice. That said; the idea is not to whizz out of your emotions and try and maintain an even keel. Our feelings are part of what makes being human so amazing. I'm just letting you know that when you've had enough of feeling a way that doesn't feel any fun to feel . . . you can stop. Keep on reading and by the end of the book you'll know lots of ways to do that easily.

I am firmly of the opinion that there is no such thing as a negative emotion. For some reason, we tend to divide them into positive and negative. I would like to suggest that you use your emotions another way. Your emotions are a support system, letting you know, "yes, more of that please" or "no thanks, I don't want any more of that." We are going to go through this in a lot more depth on Day 7 so for now, just know that any emotions you would have described in the past as negative, are just your mind, body and vibration saying, "Change something please."

The roles of your conscious and unconscious minds

As I've already described, your unconscious mind holds all the data you've ever absorbed. I like to think of the conscious mind as an interface between all that information and your current awareness. Like a computer can hold a mind-blowing amount of programs and information, but also has a screen showing you what you want to look at right now. Imagine trying to communicate with someone, or make a simple decision about what to wear if you were aware of every bit of data you have ever collected . . . it would be overwhelming!

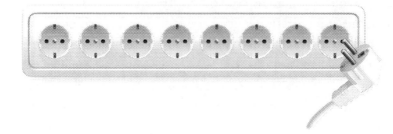

The conscious mind functions like one of the old plug and cord switchboards or a powerboard. There are a limited number of lines/plugs available for your awareness. Your unconscious mind however, is like the world's oceans—huge and vast (and some of it is dirty and polluted and some of it is pristine, beautiful and refreshing to swim in).

Check this out: I want you to start singing your national anthem in your mind, pay attention to your spine and posture and be aware of how often you're blinking . . . you can do that, right?

Now try this, keep singing (or just playing a recording of) your national anthem in your mind, paying attention to your spine and posture and how often you're blinking, but also notice the colours around you, how your clothes feel on your skin and listen for any outside sounds, make a picture in your mind of a tap-dancing elephant and take a deep breath in through your nose and see what you can smell.

What was your elephant wearing? Mine has a tutu on and is dancing up on her back legs . . . what's yours up to?

Anyway, how did you go with that second exercise? What data did you lose? Try this exercise over and over and see if you're actually able to keep track of all that stuff because you most likely forgot to keep seeing, listening, feeling or smelling some aspect of the list.

This limitation of your conscious mind is a very nifty thing to know because you can use it, on purpose, to think and therefore feel differently.

Let's imagine you have a public speaking engagement coming up and you keep having that awareness pop into one of your conscious plug holes. You're not feeling very confident about it so you take up even more plug holes making pictures of it going badly, pictures of you looking out at the uninterested crowd, pictures of yourself from the outside looking and feeling stupid, hearing your internal dialog screaming, "Say something, you're looking like a fool!" or "Shut up, you're rambling!" . . . you get the idea. The more of your plug holes you fill with this kind of imaginary input, the more you'll negatively impact your physiology (breathing, stress levels, etc.) and it's not even happening. This is the perfect time to engage your ability to choose what to fill your plug holes with. When you notice yourself in one of these kinds of situations (conscious plug holes filled with not-nice-feeling stuff) take the time firstly to take in what's around you. What can you see; what posture have you adopted? Sit or stand up straighter, take deep breaths in and notice what that does. Make a comment inside your head about the day—"what beautiful sunshine" or "imagine how happy the ducks are now" or whatever is external to you. How you think, generates how you feel, so the more stuff you notice that you can put a positive spin on the sooner you'll feel better.

This technique, while incredibly useful for reducing stress that you're imagining yourself into, does not take the place of actual planning though. If you did have a speaking engagement coming up, then plan it, have notes to take in if you need them, get the support you need and practice it lots beforehand. Be as prepared as you can be and then let it go and if it pops up into conscious awareness, then it's time to fill those plug holes with positive observations: "man, my new underpants are comfortable" or something like that. Or if you're determined to mentally rehearse your presentation, fill the plug holes with the imagination of it going really, really well and how great you'll feel, what you'll hear and see and experience as the direct result of it going as well as you can imagine.

Today's Commitment to Authentic Personal Power

As you go about the next 24 hours, I ask you to be aware, as often as you can, of how you are feeling. As you notice your feelings, and don't judge them, whatever they are, try and track back to the thinking that lead you there. Look for the conscious and the unconscious elements. The conscious being whatever you noticed happening inside your head. The unconscious being how this relates to the *program* of your experiences from the past.

If you want to take the experience one step further, you can try using the plug hole system—fill your conscious mind with new thoughts and awareness if you find yourself in a yucky feeling.

Before we go on to Day 3, take some time to reflect on what you noticed.

- What were the most common feelings you found within yourself?

- What did you notice about your thinking?

- If you tried to shift out of any unpleasant feelings, how did you go?

- How easy was it to notice other things and shift your focus?

- Did you vary what you chose to notice or was there a whole lot of songs playing inside your mind, postural awareness and blinking observation?

- What were the three most valuable observations/lessons/ realisations you've gained from taking the time to do this exercise?

  1)

  2)

  3)

Day 3

How You Feel Generates Your Responses

It really is not about what happens outside of you

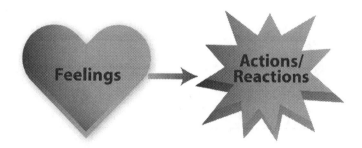

Today we're going to start by defining what's 'inside' of you and what's 'outside' of you. I realise that it may seem a bit strange and perhaps the 'inside' can easily be defined as everything on the inside of your skin; and the 'outside' everything outside of your skin. However, you'd be surprised how much we assume outside forces are responsible for things happening inside of us. For example:

- *x* makes me so angry.
- *x* makes me laugh.
- I was hit with a wave of regret (like regret is an external force coming at you).
- I fell in love (like love is a hole you can trip and fall into).
- He shocked me with his shameless behaviour!

Here's what's true: No one has the power to shock you with behavior that your *program* just doesn't find shocking.

Nobody, outside of you, can make you feel anything that you do not already have the ingredients of inside of you.

It's how you feel right now in this moment (and over time with regards to your existing *program*) that generates how you are going to react to the things going on around you.

Have you ever had someone really love you and you didn't feel the same way? There's nothing they can do about it, is there? Have you ever tried to make someone jealous, who just wasn't that kind of person? It just doesn't work, does it? Has someone ever told you a joke that they thought was riotously hilarious and you didn't think it was funny? Has someone you didn't care about at all ever insult you? It's very different to when the same thing comes out of the mouth of someone you respect, isn't it?

We are going to explore this much more deeply on Day 5—What's Real. For today, it's just important to keep in the back of your mind to be at *cause* and to own the state of being you are in as your very own creation.

Remember the exercise from Day 2, where you entered into a powerful positive memory and then a negative memory? Now imagine an annoying, repetitive sound, like a truck beeping while reversing, going on for a bit too long . . . how would you react to that if it happened in the background of your positive memory? How about in the negative one? Imagine one of the hoses coming off your washing machine and flooding the floor . . . how would the state of being you were in at the time generate your response? Whether you laugh or cry when things like this happen depends on how you feel at the time, yes?

Think about some experiences you've had where someone cuts in front of you in a line or while you're driving. There is more than likely a range of feelings you've experienced and reactions that followed.

When fully in the grip of being at *effect* we blame the outside world for the state of being we end up in. To experience just how true this is, think about daily tasks and the wildly different reactions you can have to them. Let me give you a few ideas to kick-start you.

- There's too many dirty dishes in the sink for you to get the kettle in there and fill it up.
- You are on the toilet and realise there's no paper in the place where the paper should be.
- You're going to be late because your partner isn't ready on time.
- Your children are dragging their feet getting ready for school in the morning.
- You can't find a hair tie for your hair.
- You hear the garbage truck and realise you've forgotten to put the bins out.
- You've left your phone at home.

- Someone looks at you strangely on the train.
- One of your friends makes a joke at your expense.
- There's clothes (that aren't yours) left on the floor.
- You're being held up in a parking lot because the driver blocking you is being indecisive.
- The person in front of you at the supermarket has decided to pay with coins and it's taken over five minutes so far . . .
- You put a hole in your stockings or socks putting them on.

When you're feeling happy, relaxed, content, joyful or inspired, it's quite easy to respond to all of these in a happy, relaxed, content, joyful or inspired way. When you're already feeling frustrated or a bit down in the dumps, any of these could make you flip your lid, true? How much you're nodding your head in agreement might depend on how recently you flipped-out over something you normally handle more gracefully.

Let me remake a very clear distinction—just because you erupt in a frustrating situation, when you could have responded more calmly had you been in a different state of being, does not mean that it is wrong to erupt. It does not mean that you're meant to be meandering through life putting up with substandard behaviour. You don't have to do the dishes and change the toilet rolls all the time and never say: "Hey guys, let's have a roster or something so that the distribution of household chores is fair on us all." The purpose of pointing all this out is so that you can take responsibility for how you feel and take whatever action you need to feel better. It's not the person in front of you that is paying with coins fault that you're not feeling great. It's also not their doing if you happen to enjoy the five minutes of pleasant daydreaming that their behaviour allows you to have. Remembering back to Day 2, "There is no such thing as a negative emotion," it's all just feedback. Sometimes the feedback simply is: "I'm not enjoying this!"

The main thing to remember is: When you're blaming those outside of you for how you are feeling, you're no longer at *cause*. It's your job to respect yourself. It's your job to be aware of your causes and their effects, to practice and see what gives you the results you're after. It's your job to set healthy boundaries and communicate your feelings. You are always in charge of what you choose to do inside of you. Therefore, you are in charge of your actions and reactions.

Let's say that again: You are always in charge of what you choose to do inside of you. Therefore you are in charge of your actions and reactions.

Just sit with that for a moment.

How does it feel?

Who do you want to be?

If you had access to all possible reactions to positive or challenging situations, what would you choose?

Guess what . . . you do have access to all possible reactions. Are you excited or daunted?

As you are no doubt already aware, good skills of any kind take time to acquire. If you've been reading through today and deciding to do something new, please know that the very first time you do this new thing it might not be your best work. In fact, most times when we start doing new things, we're clumsy and awkward. Go to a park and watch a toddler if you don't have one of your own. Give yourself permission to be a bit wobbly when responding in new ways and choosing to access new thoughts and feelings. It's OK to be in the learning phase. It would be a good idea to get used to it because even once you master this next new thing, you'll end up in the learning phase for the next new thing.

What if being 'perfect' was just being willing to realise you're in charge and to try out new actions?

I want for you to know that I, like most of you, have felt every emotion there is. I have been so angry that I thought I would burst (or try to burst someone else), I have been depressed, where I couldn't see that I had even one redeeming quality or access feeling positive about anything. I have felt so ugly and disgusting in my body that I didn't want anyone to see me. I have felt so afraid that sleeping with the bedroom light on was a necessity. It was all of these completely horrible feelings and my desire to feel better that lead me down the path of self—development in the first place. I am so grateful now for all the experiences that lead me to prioritise healing myself. Now that I am able to feel confidence and gratitude, I respond really differently to life. I'm sharing this so you know I didn't just dream up these tools without ever needing to use them for myself. I've written this book because I'm convinced that it will help those of you who are feeling as disconnected as I used to from how fabulous you truly are.

Today's Commitment to Authentic Personal Power

Answer these questions:

1) When you love, respect and adore yourself as the perfect work-in-progress that you are, what new feelings will you have about yourself and your life?

2) How will the way you see yourself change?

3) What kind of thoughts will you be having that make all those feelings possible?

4) When you are feeling fabulous, what new actions can you take?

5) What will immediately become possible when you take these new actions?

6) What will be the longer-term, flow-on benefits of all of these changes you've made?

Go there, day dream about it, and start feeling fabulous today! Maybe try out saying new things to yourself—choose from your answers to Question 3.

Have a wonderful, empowering day! You are totally awesome, already, just by being you and for being open to learning and growing and being even better than you were yesterday!

DAY 4

How You've Created Your 'Now'

*Beginning to understand how the past has created
what you see, hear & feel inside & all around*

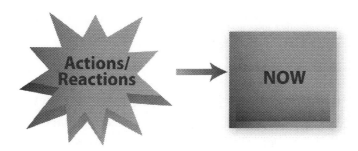

How you've spent your life, thus far, acting and reacting has generated your results—the 'now' that is your current life. So, if there's something in your current existence you're not enjoying, now is the time to celebrate that you have the building blocks for change:

1) Be at *cause* and embrace the power you have to change your mind.
2) New thinking will create new feelings.
3) These feelings will lead you to take new actions.
4) New actions generate new results.

Is it that simple?

Yes and no.

Yes, because doing the same thing you've always done will get you the same results you've always got and comparatively by doing different things you get different results.

No, because there are times when changing your thinking can be tricky (or damned near impossible) and that's why there's still over five weeks remaining on this journey you've chosen for yourself.

Today, I'm going to provide you with examples of these building blocks in action. My first story is about a client I was seeing called Andrew. His fiancé was exhibiting what he considered to be flirty behaviour with other men, including his friends, when they went out. He was very angry and these were some of the kinds of things he said to me during our first session: "She's just not what I signed up for! She's not what she seemed to be when we first met! She *never* smiles and plays with me like that! She's obviously a *total* tart! How could I not have seen what she was really like? I clearly have to break up with her if I'm to have *any* self-respect! This *always* happens to me! Life is so unfair! *All* the good women are gone! I'm going to live my *whole* life lonely and miserable!" He was 25.

All of this was without asking her, or himself, a single question.

After some good questioning, Andrew realised that he actually felt like he was out of his league with this woman. Deep down in his unconscious mind she was highlighting the "not good enough" parts of his program. This perception created several things in their relationship. Firstly, he was unconsciously preparing for their separation from the outset, not truly believing he could keep being in a relationship with a woman so wonderful. This resulted in him avoiding vulnerability by not opening up to her and stopped their relationship from deepening. Secondly, he didn't enjoy the feeling that she was out of his league, so he would focus a lot of attention on what he considered to be her 'bad' points so he felt better about himself. Thirdly, because he saw her as naturally happy and confident (which had attracted him to her in the first place) he stopped complementing her or being verbally positive with the news she'd share about her career and friendships. Furthermore, when they were out, his "not good enough" thinking made him assess every other man in the room as being a threat to him, especially if they were taller than him or he thought they were wealthier or better looking.

What do you think the relationship was like for his fiancé? What do you think the effects were of all of his causes?

Whether he was right or wrong about his fiancé being "a total tart" is beside the point in terms of the fundamental requirement for him to get in touch with being at *cause*. We can never know the "truth" about a situation without communication. And we can never test the "truth" of a situation without choosing new thoughts and actions and seeing their effects.

The first type of communication required is the internal kind. For that, let's go back to the comments Andrew made in his first session. I want to draw your attention to the italicized words: never, total, all, always, whole. These are all absolutes. There's no room for it to be any different. So, I would ask him: "Never? Really, she's *never, ever,* smiled and played with you like that?"

"*Always*? Really? When is it not that way?"

Whenever you find yourself speaking in absolutes, it's a time to ask yourself some questions and make room for change. Look for counter examples that contradict your 'always' and 'nevers'.

How we think generates how we feel. The words we use to describe things, indicates the thought programs we have in place around them.

The result of Andrew asking all these questions was an unpacking of the not-good-enough and repacking it as a worthiness work-in-progress. He learned to express his fears and his needs to the woman who loves him and has created a much happier 'now'.

I once worked with a beautiful woman named June who came to me, filled with shame, about the amount of money she'd been gambling. She called it an addiction. What does the word 'addiction' mean to you? If someone told you they had an addiction, how easily do you believe they could transform that? Is it something that would take lots of time and effort? Or could they just change their mind? What about the word 'habit'? What thoughts or images do you create in your mind around that word? In my experience, describing something as an addiction or a habit seems to be the justification for staying firmly at *effect*. The little paper cylinder filled with tobacco is stronger that I am—it's in charge and I'm at its mercy. The mindless machine or the deck of cards is more powerful than I am. The feeling of "yay!" I get when I 'win' is stronger than the "yay!" that I'm willing to create in other ways. I talked to June about what addiction meant to her and she described to me the highs and lows of her gambling experiences.

I asked June about her relationship history:

Me: "Have you ever had a partner, friend, lover or other significant relationship with someone that you really enjoyed and spent lots of time with?"

June: "Yes."

Me: "Are you still in each and every one of those relationships?"

June: "No."

Me: "Is there any relationship where a single incident forever changed your opinion (thoughts) and; therefore; feelings toward that person?

June: "Yes."

So, we unpacked what happened in those relationships that had changed and there was usually a conflict in values (fundamentally important beliefs about what's 'right' and 'wrong'). So, all I needed to was to talk some more about her relationship with gambling and have June get very clear on how this choice was actually violating her own values.

Me: "What is the positive benefit of choosing an activity that allows you to feel such deep shame?"

June: "Then I get to hate myself."

Me: "And when you hate yourself the most, you can choose that activity over and over and then keep on feeling worse and worse, right?"

June: "Yes."

Me: "So, how is that any different from choosing to harm yourself physically?"

In that moment the 'I'm-Choosing-to-Self-Harm' connection was made. She's never been even slightly tempted to gamble since.

The purpose of the client stories is to show you the direct links between: thinking—feeling—acting—reacting, thus creating your 'now'. You have created your right 'now', the parts you love and the other stuff too, with a combination of your resources from life such as: what you've been accessing from your mind, what you've been doing with your body and the quality of your energy. We're going to talk more about your body and energy later on, but for now, let's celebrate where you are 'now'. And . . . you can change anything that you're not enjoying either by a) shifting your perspective and/or b) actually shifting into new circumstances. Both of these require you to be at *cause* and follow the pathway creation and making sense of the 'now'.

Today's Commitment to Authentic Personal Power

Choose a situation from your life that you are not completely happy with and answer these questions about it:

- Where are you 'now' with this situation?

- If your 'now' could be any way at all, what would you choose?

- With all the new awareness you've gained from the last few days, do you feel you are at *cause* in this situation?

If this situation involves another person:

- Can you recognize anything you're doing that is worsening the situation?

- What could you do differently that may diffuse the situation?

- By shifting into the powerful place of *cause*; what thoughts already existed in your *program*, before this situation even began, that have allowed it to exist in your life?

- What do you believe about yourself and your life that have made it possible for you to be right here, right now?

- If there was a positive benefit for you, in having this exact situation/experience, what would it be?

- What can you learn from being right here, right now, that you couldn't have learned any other way?

- Is it OK with you to experience that learning, now, and make a new choice that will allow this situation to change, right now?

- What new thoughts about that old situation are available to you now?

- What new feelings are you now able to access from shifting your point of thinking and focus?

- What are some new actions, behaviours, and responses you will have, as a direct result of that new thinking?

- Do you now feel at *cause* for making these changes?

- How great does that feel?

If you're feeling some kind of wonderful, that's fabulous. If you're not, please don't throw the book away! On Day 16, we're going to look at *Blurk*—Feeling Down, Dark and Unmotivated. So keep on reading, learn the basics and by the time we get to Day 16, all kinds of new perspectives will be possible—I promise!

What's Real?

How you interpret the world around you
based on what you already believe to be true

Did you know that you interpret the world around you based on what you already believe to be true?

I come across many people, who pride themselves on being open-minded, but in reality it's a skill-set that very few have mastered and here's why: no one can know what they don't know. If I were to veer off English now and finish this book using a language you haven't learned, would you be able to continue learning from the content? No.

In the exact same way, if you are ridiculously good looking and are used to people constantly drooling in your direction, you're very able to notice this going on around you. Likewise, if you consider yourself to be hideously ugly, I'm sure you've seen people around you noticing that, too. Am I right so far?

Well, here's the thing: You are the meaning-maker of your world. And as the meaning-maker, you are constantly re-affirming what you already believe to be true. Your unconscious mind loves you and has a special department I like to call, the *Proover Department*. Just like vehicle developers have a proving ground to test out new cars, your unconscious mind has thinking departments including the *Proover Department* which likes to prove you correct.

We have all had experiences with people and their pre-existing beliefs. I was in a bar one night and a very confident, young Italian man sauntered up to me and informed me that I was welcome to go home and spend the night with him. When I laughed and said, "No, thanks," the look on his face was one I interpreted as puzzled. He asked me, "Are you a lesbian?" I use this story as an example because I imagine his unconscious program had no reference point for a heterosexual woman *not* wanting him. In contrast, I met one of my friends one night when, after a few drinks, I crossed the crowded room to tell him that I thought he was very handsome. He had no unconscious reference for that possibly being true and so assumed it was a practical joke and that one of the people he was out with had put me up to it.

Looking at this picture, what do you interpret this look to mean?

Is he thinking:

"You are such an idiot!"
"What would you know you old fogie?"
or "hmmm, I'd like to rip your pants off?"

If this young man happened to be looking at you, how would you interpret that look? It's going to depend on what you already believe, isn't it? If he was looking that way at a friend of yours, what would you take his look mean? It's going to depend on the friend you chose to think of and what you already think of them isn't it?

Most of the time, we actually have very little idea what's going on in other people's minds. How often have you met someone, quite convinced of their self-esteem, only to find out later on that they were nervous at the time of meeting you?

You are the *meaning maker* in your world

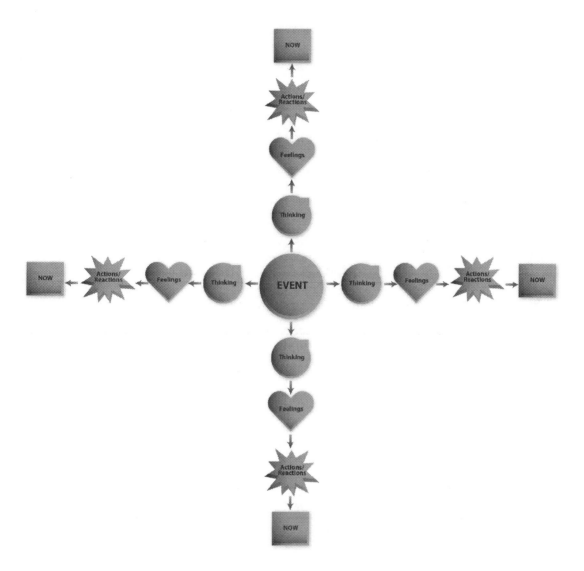

Most events are actually neutral. Whether they become interpreted as 'positive' or 'negative' depends on the existing beliefs of the person doing the interpreting. The specific interpretation of the 'positive' or 'negative' event likewise depends on the existing beliefs of the person having the experience. All of these accumulative actions and reactions create the 'now'.

I have worked with many couples over the years. One of the issues that arise, every single time, is how each person in the relationship interprets the other's behaviour.

Let's see this in action:

Imagine the event in the centre of the diagram above is: Max, who is normally home by 6pm every weeknight, has come home late from work four times in the last two weeks. This occurance, in and of itself, is neutral—it's just data. That event is then interpreted by Max's partner who may think the following:

1. It's our anniversary soon; I bet Max is doing overtime so that he can take me away somewhere beautiful.
2. #%@&! Max might have been in an accident, maybe he's dead on the side of the road (this would happen each and every one of the four times).
3. Max is having an affair.
4. Max doesn't want to come home because I'm fat, ugly and boring.

These are interpretations that all come from actual clients I've worked with. The purpose of pointing all this out is *NOT* to say that you are always wrong. It is to give you a framework that has the power to free you forever from the self-constructed misery of living in the effect of unpleasant reactions.

After the interpretation, (thinking) comes the feeling and then the action/reaction when Max walks in the door. Have a think about them and fill in some answers. What would Max's partner feel as a result of each interpretation and what reaction/action would Max be on the receiving end of when he walks in the door?

1) It's our anniversary soon; I bet Max is doing overtime so that he can take me away somewhere beautiful.

   Feelings—

   Action/Reaction—

2) #%@&! Max might have been in an accident; maybe he's dead on the side of the road

Feelings—

Action/Reaction—

3) Max is having an affair.

Feelings—

Action/Reaction—

4) Max doesn't want to come home because I'm fat, ugly and boring.

Feelings—

Action/Reaction—

Have you ever been in a similar situation where someone has arrived unexpectedly late, several times in a short period? If you haven't, try and imagine it, and if so . . . what would you make it mean?

Interpretation—

What were/are the feelings that interpretation created?—

How did you act/react as a result of feeling that way?—

Let's try another one. The neutral event is: Rodney is out at dinner with Bron, his new partner, meeting her best girlfriend for the first time. During dinner the friend is really quiet and doesn't ask him any questions. Here are some interpretations of what Rodney might be thinking:

1) She must be very shy.
2) She thinks that Bron could do so much better/she doesn't approve/she doesn't like me.
3) She thinks that I don't like her.
4) She's obviously got a lot going on personally and is distracted, thinking about all of that inside her mind.

Think about the differences in feelings that these thoughts would create and; therefore, the differences in actions. Play around with these and be Rodney for a moment:

1) She must be very shy.

Feelings—

Action/Reaction—

2) She thinks that Bron could do so much better/she doesn't approve/she doesn't like me.

Feelings—

Action/Reaction—

3) She thinks that I don't like her.

Feelings—

Action/Reaction—

4) She's obviously got a lot going on personally and is distracted, thinking about all of that inside her mind.

Feelings—

Action/Reaction—

Have you ever been introduced to someone that you want to make a good impression on and they've been really quiet? What meaning did you create for it?

Interpretation—

Feelings—

Actions/Reactions—

However we end up acting and reacting is another neutral event that the other people involved are going to interpret and create feelings and reactions to.

Why is this useful to be aware of?

Do you know how totally refreshing it can be to give yourself permission to be completely wrong? It's almost like we're taught that being right is best; therefore, we need the other person to be wrong. It can be confronting to realise just how often you've been blaming the outside world for what ultimately was just your pre-existing *program*. It can also be a wonderful relief to get into *cause* and change your mind about some things and upgrade your meaning-making to something that automatically will upgrade the feelings you generate.

When you make a mistake—what do you make that mean?

When someone doesn't return you phone call—what do you make that mean?

When you step on the scales (If you happen to be into the notion of weighing yourself)—what do you make that number you see mean?

If you ask someone out on a date and they say no—what do you make that mean?

What if everything from today and the last four days of reading this book just merged together in an epiphany that made you feel totally in charge of your life . . . what would you make *that* mean?

Whatever you make it mean will be the deciding force that determines the feelings you have and the action you choose to take.

Today's Commitment to Authentic Personal Power:

One:

Take an event that is still bothering you right now. It can be something that someone said, a tone someone used with you, a situation you're involved in, a current or recently ended relationship, anything at all that still creates unpleasant feelings when you think about it.

Put that event in the middle of the, "You are the meaning-maker in your world" diagram and make it neutral (even if it doesn't feel neutral to you!). Off to one side, put the interpretation you currently have and then track out the feelings and how you're acting and reacting when those feelings come up.

Then, force yourself to come up with three other interpretations. Put yourself in each situation and think of the feelings the particular interpretation would create and what actions or reactions those feelings would cause.

Here's an example:

I was retrenched from my job and I thought the following:

1) I am a loser that's too old to be useful.

  And during the exercise, here are the other three interpretations I dreamed up—

2) Something better must be out there for me and this door had to close for the next to open.
3) It must be time for me to do the traveling I always dreamed of.
4) I've missed out on so much time with my family in that old job; this is the perfect opportunity to work in a new way that gives me more work/life balance.

Knowing that I am a thinker with a *proving department*, think of the data I could start paying attention to with my 2nd, 3rd or 4th interpretation, rather than my first.

Two:

As you go about the next 24 hours try and be aware of the meanings that you're making. Have a way of recording your thoughts (e.g. notepaper/phone with 'notes' app) and write down the noteworthy ones.

Three:

Make some time to revisit them and see how many you can put in the neutral position in the middle and what other interpretations might be possible.

Before we start with Day 6, please go back and make sure that you worked with at least three different interpretations, (if you haven't, make the time to do it now).

When you forced your events into the middle, 'neutral space', what new possibilities did you create?

What patterns did you notice?

How empowered did you feel that you were able to get your *proover* looking for new data?

DAY 6

Empowered Communication

How to own your 'stuff' and still talk about how you feel

How would you currently rate your communication skills? I'm not talking about sitting-in-a-meeting communication skills, or I'd-like-to-buy-that-washing-machine-please communication skills. I *am* talking about the skills you are currently using to talk about how you feel with the people in your life that truly matter to you.

In my work, I've come across two main issues with communication. The first is people not communicating their feelings at all. This group lets all their interpretations and feelings build up and up. They imagine when they communicate their feelings or express their needs that it's going to create a huge argument. In their imagination, it is all going to be horrible, so they let it build up and up some more . . . sound familiar?

The other group is much more forceful (but still most certainly at effect). This is the I AM TELLING YOU RIGHT NOW HOW YOU'VE MADE ME FEEL, IT'S ALL YOUR FAULT, I AM RIGHT AND YOU ARE WRONG AND YOU BETTER START DOING SOMETHING ELSE RIGHT NOW group.

Interestingly, these groups often end up in relationships with each other and perpetuate each other's patterns.

Whichever group you happen to fall into, today is going to be enlightening. That said, many people can do a bit of both, depending on the situation, so you're not wholly one or the other, but capable of everything from one end of the spectrum to the other.

The first thing I want to talk about today is about getting you into *cause* with your communication skills. Please take a moment to acknowledge how well you've trained the people around you to behave the way they do. If you imagine that people are going to be cross with you for talking with them about how you feel, so you back right off as soon as they get cross . . . what do you think the effect of that is long-term? You may have trained those around you to think that if

39

they get cross you'll realise they're right, and you were wrong. If you are excellent at repeatedly telling people how wrong they are and how much that wrongness is hurting you then what do you think the effect of that is long-term? You've probably trained those around you to stop communicating with you to avoid your reaction. Neither way is easily generating heart-felt communication and understanding.

Pop Quiz:

So, first things first, if you want a new result, who is in charge of making that happen?

If you've automatically answered: "I am"—you pass with flying colours.

The one difference between blaming and expression is the part where you take responsibility for your interpretation and the emotions you've created. I know this may contradict most of your previous *programming*, but it's really important to remember that you do create all your own feelings. When someone gives you flowers you can make it mean they've done something wrong that they're not telling you about and feel suspicious; or you can make it mean that they love and appreciate you and feel wonderfully acknowledged.

Let me take you through an example of expression. We'll use my Max example, from Day 5—What's Real? Here are examples of conversations Max's partner could have with him to address the issues she is facing:

1) You know how over the last couple of weeks you've come home later than usual a few times? Well, every time, I've been making it mean that something might have happened to you and I've ended up making myself all worried, then anxious and eventually built up to becoming totally frantic. Would you mind doing something for me? Could you message me when you're going to be late? It's not that you're doing anything wrong; it's just that, at the moment, it would really help me to be totally relaxed and probably a lot more fun to walk in the door to.

2) You know how over the last couple of weeks you've come home later than usual a few times? Well, in my head I've gone into the possibility that you might be seeing someone else. I'm not saying I'm right, that's just where I've gone in my mind. And then, with that thought I can end up looking for proof to confirm my fear and that's such a horrible place to live in. I'm not accusing you, but I just needed to share where my head's gone and what I'm doing to myself so that if you see weird behaviour, it will

make sense. Can we make some time to talk about 'us' because I need your help to work through this?

3) You know how over the last couple of weeks you've come home later than usual a few times? Well, I've been watching that and inside my own mind, I've made it mean that maybe you don't want to come home anymore. With that thinking I've made myself feel all hurt and rejected. I think I've interpreted it that way because I'm not feeling very good about my body, I feel overweight and I imagine you think that, too, and because I feel yuck about myself, I don't really want to go out as much, so maybe I'm being really boring. And my deepest fear that comes up when I'm thinking and feeling all of that it is that maybe, you don't want to be married to me anymore. I can't go on having these fears and not talking with you about it. I need reassurance or we need to make a plan to improve our relationship.

Let me give you another example, from the couple I talked about on Day 1—Cause & Effect. Sarah was experiencing bursts of rage with her partner and suppressing it all by taking responsibility for her feelings, but without communicating with her husband. She was feeling very alone in the parenting of their son, misunderstood and unsupported by her husband. She had gone from being a successful professional earning as much money as her husband to being at home with their child. Her husband continued to work, play sport, socialise with his friends, relax in the evenings watching TV—all the things that he'd done prior to becoming a father. Sarah on the other hand was experiencing a day-to-day reality that was unrecognisable to her life pre-motherhood. While she had chosen to be a stay-at-home mother, she was really angry that the household chores were all hers and her ability to have a sporty or social life had also altered. After learning these tools with me she went home and expressed her feelings in a new and empowering way.

"Josh, I have got to talk with you about some stuff that I've got going on inside my head. My thoughts are making all kinds of feelings that aren't any fun and I'm feeling disconnected from you as a result. You know how you're still playing hockey on the weekends, training and catching up with your mates and how when I asked you the other night if I could catch up with Sue you said you really needed a night of no baby-stress to just chill out on the couch? And I ended up staying home? Well, in my head I've interpreted that as you thinking I'm 100% responsible for parenting our son, and that parenting for you is an optional activity that you can say 'yes' or 'no' to, and it doesn't feel like I've got the same options. When I think that way, it makes me feel really angry and frustrated and I've been holding that in and shutting you out emotionally. I really need to get clear on what we both want from each other, what both our roles are with this beautiful baby we chose to have, so that we are both having our needs met."

She then apologised for being shut down and blocking him out, instead of just talking with him about how she was feeling.

Do you think this style of communication is more likely to generate a useful conversation and sharing of thoughts and feelings than if she would have said, "YOU ARE SO SELFISH! I'm so sick of you leaving me to do EVERYTHING while you just kick back with your feet up!"?

No one can respond to how they affect you if you don't share with them what's going on inside your mind.

Here are some steps to follow for empowered emotional communication:

1) State the neutral event.
2) Take responsibility for your interpretation, owning the possibility that you may not be correct.
3) Share how your thinking has made you feel i.e. what has your interpretation brought up for you.
4) Understand that the other person will be listening, interpreting, and feeling all their stuff as well, so allow the process all the time it needs. Just because you've learned to express today, doesn't mean everyone else will instantly do it the same way.
5) If you have a sense of what you need, be willing to directly ask for it.

Now, be very honest with yourself, what comes up when you read through these examples? To communicate in this way requires vulnerability and surrender of 'rightness' and 'wrongness', doesn't it?

How would you feel, being this open and at *cause* for your feelings and behaviours?

Do you fear that if you communicated your feelings in this way that the other person would happily just blame you for what you've done in your head and take no action to change things?

If yes, what state are your relationships actually in?

In the case of Sarah, her husband had a total shift in attitude and behaviour after she expressed herself without blaming him. He was hurt that she'd been feeling angry and disconnected and had lied to him by saying everything was OK. They continued to use this communication tool to be vulnerable with each other and their relationship deepened into a whole new place. Practically, they now co-ordinate activities outside of family life together so that each parent gets time-out for sport and fun and they plan in family time and couple time, too. He had been feeling as though their son was more important to Sarah than he was and hadn't expressed that correctly, so when he did, things were able to change there, too.

Please know that you can never really know what kind of relationship you are in until you allow that person to truly know you. For that to happen, you must be willing to communicate, without blame, by owning your interpretations and expressing your feelings. For most of you, this will be a brand new skill. Like all skills, they are mastered with trial and correction, so just start trialling and correcting as you go. You can be upfront with the people in your life and tell them you are trying out some new tools for expressing yourself so when you sound completely different to them, they won't wonder if there is a hidden camera hidden somewhere.

The purpose of expressing yourself is so that you are not suppressing your emotions. Suppressed emotions sit in your body and energy—building up, until they explode out *somewhere* and not always in the way you'd like. It will cause stress. Stress is the major cause of disease. This book is teaching you how your mind, body and energy work together to create empowerment, and how learning to express your feelings is really important for wholistic health and vitality. As you get better and better at remembering to express your feelings, you will see that new choices become available. There will be some relationships that deepen and grow with shared understanding and there will be others that go in the opposite direction. There will be habitual interpretations that show you the next area to focus on in your personal development and this is what I'll be covering next. If you have habitually suppressed your emotions and you get really good at choosing to use this tool instead, you'll feel so much lighter and freer to feel the wonderful feelings that are available to you. Your relationships will feel more wonderful, too, and when someone says, "I love you," you'll be able to absorb it into the depth that you've shared.

Try it and see.

There are lots of different kinds of relationships, too, and you get to choose which ones you have. Not every relationship has to be totally vulnerable and deep, unless you want it that way. However, if you want to be understood, known and loved for whom you are; then you need to be willing to use the tools you're learning today.

Today's Commitment to Authentic Personal Power

1) Choose something that you've been upset about, in one of your relationships. Have a think about what the neutral event was and what you've made it mean.

2) Following the steps outlined today, write down an expression. Make sure that at no point you are blaming the other person for the feelings that you've had as a result of your own thinking. Practice it out loud, several times.

How does it feel after doing that?

Next, contact the person and let them know that you've been learning new ways to communicate your feelings and tell them that you want to share. Follow the steps and share the expression you've been practicing. If this is something that's outside of your comfort zone, don't choose the most significant relationship of your life; instead practice with a friend or someone you feel a bit safer with. Many of my clients struggle with conveying their wording in a way they feel really happy with so feel free ask someone to help you. Just make sure you follow the steps, be at *cause* and then . . . do it!

And remember—to get *new* results you need to take *new* actions.

Before we start with Day 7—make some notes about your experiences. It will be really fun to go back to these notes in six months and see just how far you've come!

How was your first empowered expression?

What will you do the same next time?

What will you do differently next time?

What are some of the events and who are some of the people you will use this tool to express about/to in the future?

What would it be like for you, mentally, physically and energetically if you were able to easily talk about your feelings without needing to squish them down and ignore them?

In the spirit of being at *cause* also know that just because you have this tool doesn't mean you need to use it every time you have a feeling. I have fabulous black boots that keep my feet nice and warm, it doesn't mean that I have to wear them every day or that they are appropriate for all weather conditions and all occasions. There are times when you have a reaction to something and you can just own it and process it all on your own. The way to tell in these beginning stages whether you need to express or not, is whether it's hanging around and pestering you like an insect trapped inside your brain. If your reaction is hanging around, express it, or talk with someone else about these tools and practice an expression. You'll know by doing this practice, whether you need to do it with the person involved or not.

Intense Reactions as Goal Posts for Your Next Step

Why getting hurt and angry can be a powerful and useful thing to do

During Day 6 we learned wonderful tools for communicating in an empowered way. Today we're going to talk about giving yourself permission to totally lose it, get mad, get loud and have intense reactions. These reactions do not have to be directed at another person. The point is to allow yourself to have intense reactions because it's actually a very good way to experience how you truly feel.

Where are you on the spectrum?

a) I never want to upset anybody so I avoid confrontation and don't ever share my feelings if it might cause an upset.

b) I can talk about how I feel, but only if it's really, really important, I try and get through as much as I can inside myself without letting it show.

c) I talk about how I feel when I need to, but I always try to do it in an even tone and stay quite controlled with expressing myself.

d) I can talk about how I feel. If it's a really strong feeling then I can get loud or sob while I'm doing it.

e) I'm all over the place, sometimes I share, sometimes I don't. Sometimes I'm rational about it and sometimes I'm hysterical or it can be anywhere in-between.

f) I explode all the time, I never keep anything in. No one's ever left wondering, I just put it all out there.

Where ever you are on the spectrum, your emotions are a guidance system and it's really important that you pay attention to them.

For those of you in the e) to f) range, you may be surrounded by people who are more a) to c) so this might be interesting for you to read for yourself and with them in mind.

When was the last time you got really mad? You know, even when you reach the highest levels of personal development, you still have a heart that can be hurt and values that can be violated and situations, people, and events that can highlight anger inside of you. The difference is how long it takes for you to take action, express yourself, see the positives and move on. Your feelings are a very powerful guidance system that gives you instant feedback on the quality of your thinking and the quality of your circumstances. Being upset and choosing to keep it inside rarely changes anything. Being upset and huffing about something, but not sharing how you truly feel, will only create misinterpretation. Being upset and communicating it with the same amount of energy as the upset will release the charge of it—even if you're just communicating with yourself.

When I look back over my life, many of the fantastic transformations I chose to embark upon happened after I hit a rock-bottom place and got really emotional about it. Screaming out to the Universe, "AAAHHH I'M SO SICK OF THIS!" is a wonderful way to release pressure and a powerful place to make new choices that correct the situation. Long before I learned the tools of empowered communication, my anger and hurt would build and build and would result in me terminating relationships (without ever expressing) or having an explosion. In some cases I had built up such a wall during my silence that the relationship wasn't repairable. I was so immersed in *effect* that I wanted the other person to notice that I wasn't OK and the fact that they didn't meant they didn't care—what a stunning method of taking no personal responsibility. I stayed quiet to avoid confrontation, but I wasn't actually doing anyone any favours. In other cases, the explosion was a wonderful release of emotional pressure because I finally shared how I was feeling and the other person heard me, understood where I was coming from, and together we made changes.

Have you known an often-angry person who, when pushed to extreme anger can become quiet? It has more of an impact, doesn't it, as opposed to when they just do the regular shouting? When a normally peaceful and quiet person loses it loudly, it has more of an impact, too. The same is true internally (not just what the outside world sees). If you normally explain your intense reactions away then try, in the safety of your own company, to allow the feelings to rush through you—they are there for a reason.

In essence, be willing to do something new to create newness. Your emotions are a guidance system that helps you move towards positive change.

Today I say to you:

If you normally suppress your feelings then: Stop letting things simmer!! You deserve to be happy and content. If you normally express all of your feelings, without regard for the impact you have then today, take a moment to stop and use the Empowered Communication tools. You, too, deserve for your feelings to be given the attention you crave. Using new methods of communicating will create newness.

Everyone deserves to have goals and be excited about achieving them, because you can and you will when you take the right actions. You deserve to be loved and adored, heard, known and understood. You deserve to love and adore, listen, know, and understand. You deserve to feel connected to all that you are and feel the power of being a meaningful and important part of the whole.

Today's Commitment to Authentic Personal Power

1) What's brewing?

Think about the areas of your life in the following six broad categories and make a note of any people or situations that have an element you're simmering about.

Work:

Finances:

Health:

Personal Development/Spirituality:

Community:

Relationships:

Pick one and make a choice today to hit the "THAT'S ENOUGH!" place.

What action can you take in the next 24 hours that you know will begin to make the changes you desire?

2) Listening:

What does it take for you to stop, listen and really hear what the people around you are sharing?

When someone shares with you, do you take the time to understand their point of view (whether you agree or not) or do you bombard them with your own stuff?

Is it hard for you to respect people that avoid confrontation and are submissive in their interactions with you?

Do you want to change any of that?

What could you choose, right now, that would begin that change?

3) Setting your intention:

If you were able to choose your communication style and level of skill, how would you like to be able to relate to others?

How would you like to be able to set boundaries that honour you and communicate them easily?

How would you like to be when listening to the responses to you're receiving?

What would you like the final end result to be? If you could easily communicate in the way you've described, how would you feel about yourself, your relationships and your life?

DAY 8

Self-Assessment Day (#1)

Fill in this survey to see where you're at right now

Today is your first Self-Assessment Day. You've been reading all about your mind and have probably already had several significant realisations about your *program*. You may have even started making some changes that will create permanent positive benefits in your life. Don't worry if you haven't yet; you first need to realise that life could be better and secondly that you are capable of making new choices and decisions necessary to improve your 'now'.

Today we are going to get very clear about what's deep inside you. We all have dark corners of our unconscious minds where we keep all the stuff we'd rather not look at. The thing is, your beautiful and very intelligent unconscious mind, would love for you to be as happy and as healthy as you can possibly be. Therefore, some mental spring cleaning is now in order. Today's the part where you take everything out of the cupboards and have a look at it, dust it off if necessary and choose what to chuck out and what to keep. It's OK for this phase of spring cleaning to be a bit messy. We will clean it up tomorrow and keep on cleaning throughout the next 34 days.

Today's Commitment to Authentic Personal Power

The ideal scenario is for you to be able to complete the following exercise in a quiet place, on your own, away from distractions and where it's OK for emotions to burst out. You may not experience a stream of emotions, but if you do, you might prefer not to be in the lunch room at work or in front of someone whom you wouldn't choose to share your deeper feelings with.

The following is a list of words or sentences, activities, states of mind, behaviours, emotions and concepts. Please read the word or words and write down the very first thing that comes to your mind. You are in the process of allowing your unconscious mind, your gut instincts, your innate wisdom to communicate with you and its response will be instant. Any thinking, assessing and questioning you do after your initial response is conscious interference, so please, get the first response down, even if it seems to make no conscious sense whatsoever. If the word means multiple things to you, then blurt it all out.

Are you ready?

Please remember, there are no right or wrong answers. It's OK to wish that you felt differently, because you can make that happen. This is not a test, and your answers are private so don't hide anything, please! You can answer with a single word or a whole heap of words—just make sure it's whatever comes FIRST into your mind.

Ask yourself; what are my current thoughts and beliefs about:

(Make a mark next to the ones that have a big emotional charge for you)

O Health _____

_____

O Spirituality _____

_____

O Personal development _____

_____

O Family

_____

O Money

_____

O Relationships

_____

O Feminine power

_____

O Masculine power

_____

O Community

_____

O Love

_____

O Sex

_____

O Exercise

_____

O Getting what I want

_____

O Failure

O Sickness

O Pain

O I am worthy

O I belong

O Human beings

O Abundance

O We are all created equal

O Intimacy

O Making love

O Marriage

_____

O Mother

_____

O Father

_____

O Brother

_____

O Sister

_____

O Daughter

_____

O Son

_____

O Husband

_____

O Wife

_____

O Ex-partner

_____

O Self Esteem

O Failure

O How others see me

O What others think of me

O Procrastination

O I am beautiful

O I am wanted

O I am loved

O I am tolerated

O Saying "Yes"

O I'm unlovable

_____

O I'm not good enough

_____

O I am amazing

_____

O Personal power

_____

O Coming first

_____

O Manifestation

_____

O Debt

_____

O Planet Earth

_____

O My diet

_____

O Anger

_____

O Sadness

O Fear

O Hurt

O Guilt

O I am successful

O Saying "No"

O Contributing

O Being vulnerable

O Friends

O Honesty

O Intelligence

_____

O I am clever

_____

O I am worthy

_____

O I am enough

_____

O I am a meaningful part of the whole

_____

Phew. You made it! How many of the above have marks next to them? Were you surprised by some of your reactions?

I want you to just sit with whatever has come up. On Day 9—Choosing New Beliefs, we are going to go back through the list and continue the process of creating some new beliefs.

Day 9

Choosing New Beliefs

Using the self assessment process to
continue creating new beliefs

Today we are going to make use of the work you put in yesterday. The process is simple. We take the gut response from yesterday and stepping into the empowerment of *cause*, decide what you would prefer to think or believe instead. Please know that I'm not suggesting that this, alone, magically makes you believe something new. It is however, a very powerful beginning. The final question you ask yourself is this: "What would I need to know/see/feel was true about me and about life for this to be my new thought/belief?"

Here is an example:

Love

Old thoughts/belief: Never get loved in return; I'm a fool, is it ever really real?

New thoughts/belief: I allow deep, true love into my life. I easily love myself and others.

What I would need to know/see/feel was true about me and about life for this to be my new belief: That I am totally worthy of being adored and capable of openly loving. That true love, passion, commitment and friendship exists in intimate relationships and are possible for me. It's safe to share all that I am.

There are several benefits of going through this process. It's going to take some time, so I want for you to know why you're doing it.

Firstly, it will get your mind focused on what you want to create. Thinking in this manner will create more enjoyable feelings.

Secondly, it will open up communication with your unconscious beliefs. Just like you can't start speaking Russian just by deciding you want to (without the learning process), you also can't start thinking in a new way without there being a framework inside you to make that happen.

And, thirdly, you can't decide to think in a new way when you are unaware of where the problem is. Today will provide some new insights into your unconscious responses and programming and with awareness, comes the ability to choose something new.

Now, please go through this list again and really assess, what would be the most fun new thoughts and beliefs to have? What beliefs would most honour you and your goals for life? And what would you need to personally believe about yourself for these new beliefs to easily be a daily truth in the new fabulous life you're creating now?

Today's Commitment to Authentic Personal Power

Look at yesterday's list and work with all the ones that you have put a mark against. Make sure you work with at least 20 of the words or statements. Not all words or statements will be impactful. For example, going through this process myself, the word 'brother' only brought up my childhood desire to have one. There is no need for me in this instance to work with new thoughts or beliefs. That said, often something will come up where you least expect it, so it is well worth going through them all (even if it's just mentally) and seeing what answers pop into your awareness. Take the extra step of writing down the answers for at least 20 and definitely all the ones that surprised you or brought up emotions.

<u>Health</u>

Old thoughts/belief:

New thoughts/belief:

What I would need to know/see/feel was true about me and about life for this to be my new belief:

Spirituality

Old thoughts/belief:

New thoughts/belief:

What I would need to know/see/feel was true about me and about life for this to be my new belief:

Personal development

Old thoughts/belief:

New thoughts/belief:

What I would need to know/see/feel was true about me and about life for this to be my new belief:

Family

Old thoughts/belief:

New thoughts/belief:

What I would need to know/see/feel was true about me and about life for this to be my new belief:

Money

Old thoughts/belief:

New thoughts/belief:

What I would need to know/see/feel was true about me and about life for this to be my new belief:

Relationships

Old thoughts/belief:

New thoughts/belief:

What I would need to know/see/feel was true about me and about life for this to be my new belief:

Feminine power

Old thoughts/belief:

New thoughts/belief:

What I would need to know/see/feel was true about me and about life for this to be my new belief:

Masculine power

Old thoughts/belief:

New thoughts/belief:

What I would need to know/see/feel was true about me and about life for this to be my new belief:

Community

Old thoughts/belief:

New thoughts/belief:

What I would need to know/see/feel was true about me and about life for this to be my new belief:

Love

Old thoughts/belief:

New thoughts/belief:

What I would need to know/see/feel was true about me and about life for this to be my new belief:

Sex

Old thoughts/belief:

New thoughts/belief:

What I would need to know/see/feel was true about me and about life for this to be my new belief:

Exercise

Old thoughts/belief:

New thoughts/belief:

What I would need to know/see/feel was true about me and about life for this to be my new belief:

Getting what I want

Old thoughts/belief:

New thoughts/belief:

What I would need to know/see/feel was true about me and about life for this to be my new belief:

Failure

Old thoughts/belief:

New thoughts/belief:

What I would need to know/see/feel was true about me and about life for this to be my new belief:

Sickness

Old thoughts/belief:

New thoughts/belief:

What I would need to know/see/feel was true about me and about life for this to be my new belief:

Pain

Old thoughts/belief:

New thoughts/belief:

What I would need to know/see/feel was true about me and about life for this to be my new belief:

I am worthy

Old thoughts/belief:

New thoughts/belief:

What I would need to know/see/feel was true about me and about life for this to be my new belief:

I belong

Old thoughts/belief:

New thoughts/belief:

What I would need to know/see/feel was true about me and about life for this to be my new belief:

Human beings

Old thoughts/belief:

New thoughts/belief:

What I would need to know/see/feel was true about me and about life for this to be my new belief:

Abundance

Old thoughts/belief:

New thoughts/belief:

What I would need to know/see/feel was true about me and about life for this to be my new belief:

We are all created equal

Old thoughts/belief:

New thoughts/belief:

What I would need to know/see/feel was true about me and about life for this to be my new belief:

Intimacy

Old thoughts/belief:

New thoughts/belief:

What I would need to know/see/feel was true about me and about life for this to be my new belief:

Making love

Old thoughts/belief:

New thoughts/belief:

What I would need to know/see/feel was true about me and about life for this to be my new belief:

Marriage

Old thoughts/belief:

New thoughts/belief:

What I would need to know/see/feel was true about me and about life for this to be my new belief:

Mother

Old thoughts/belief:

New thoughts/belief:

What I would need to know/see/feel was true about me and about life for this to be my new belief:

Father

Old thoughts/belief:

New thoughts/belief:

What I would need to know/see/feel was true about me and about life for this to be my new belief:

Brother

Old thoughts/belief:

New thoughts/belief:

What I would need to know/see/feel was true about me and about life for this to be my new belief:

Sister

Old thoughts/belief:

New thoughts/belief:

What I would need to know/see/feel was true about me and about life for this to be my new belief:

Daughter

Old thoughts/belief:

New thoughts/belief:

What I would need to know/see/feel was true about me and about life for this to be my new belief:

Son

Old thoughts/belief:

New thoughts/belief:

What I would need to know/see/feel was true about me and about life for this to be my new belief:

Husband

Old thoughts/belief:

New thoughts/belief:

What I would need to know/see/feel was true about me and about life for this to be my new belief:

Wife

Old thoughts/belief:

New thoughts/belief:

What I would need to know/see/feel was true about me and about life for this to be my new belief:

Ex-partner

Old thoughts/belief:

New thoughts/belief:

What I would need to know/see/feel was true about me and about life for this to be my new belief:

Self esteem

Old thoughts/belief:

New thoughts/belief:

What I would need to know/see/feel was true about me and about life for this to be my new belief:

Failure

Old thoughts/belief:

New thoughts/belief:

What I would need to know/see/feel was true about me and about life for this to be my new belief:

How others see me

Old thoughts/belief:

New thoughts/belief:

What I would need to know/see/feel was true about me and about life for this to be my new belief:

What others think of me

Old thoughts/belief:

New thoughts/belief:

What I would need to know/see/feel was true about me and about life for this to be my new belief:

Procrastination

Old thoughts/belief:

New thoughts/belief:

What I would need to know/see/feel was true about me and about life for this to be my new belief:

I am beautiful

Old thoughts/belief:

New thoughts/belief:

What I would need to know/see/feel was true about me and about life for this to be my new belief:

I am wanted

Old thoughts/belief:

New thoughts/belief:

What I would need to know/see/feel was true about me and about life for this to be my new belief:

I am loved

Old thoughts/belief:

New thoughts/belief:

What I would need to know/see/feel was true about me and about life for this to be my new belief:

I am tolerated

Old thoughts/belief:

New thoughts/belief:

What I would need to know/see/feel was true about me and about life for this to be my new belief:

Saying "yes"

Old thoughts/belief:

New thoughts/belief:

What I would need to know/see/feel was true about me and about life for this to be my new belief:

I'm unlovable

Old thoughts/belief:

New thoughts/belief:

What I would need to know/see/feel was true about me and about life for this to be my new belief:

I'm not good enough

Old thoughts/belief:

New thoughts/belief:

What I would need to know/see/feel was true about me and about life for this to be my new belief:

I am amazing

Old thoughts/belief:

New thoughts/belief:

What I would need to know/see/feel was true about me and about life for this to be my new belief:

Personal power

Old thoughts/belief:

New thoughts/belief:

What I would need to know/see/feel was true about me and about life for this to be my new belief:

Coming first

Old thoughts/belief:

New thoughts/belief:

What I would need to know/see/feel was true about me and about life for this to be my new belief:

Manifestation

Old thoughts/belief:

New thoughts/belief:

What I would need to know/see/feel was true about me and about life for this to be my new belief:

Debt

Old thoughts/belief:

New thoughts/belief:

What I would need to know/see/feel was true about me and about life for this to be my new belief:

Planet Earth

Old thoughts/belief:

New thoughts/belief:

What I would need to know/see/feel was true about me and about life for this to be my new belief:

My diet

Old thoughts/belief:

New thoughts/belief:

What I would need to know/see/feel was true about me and about life for this to be my new belief:

Anger

Old thoughts/belief:

New thoughts/belief:

What I would need to know/see/feel was true about me and about life for this to be my new belief:

Sadness

Old thoughts/belief:

New thoughts/belief:

What I would need to know/see/feel was true about me and about life for this to be my new belief:

Fear

Old thoughts/belief:

New thoughts/belief:

What I would need to know/see/feel was true about me and about life for this to be my new belief:

Hurt

Old thoughts/belief:

New thoughts/belief:

What I would need to know/see/feel was true about me and about life for this to be my new belief:

Guilt

Old thoughts/belief:

New thoughts/belief:

What I would need to know/see/feel was true about me and about life for this to be my new belief:

I am successful

Old thoughts/belief:

New thoughts/belief:

What I would need to know/see/feel was true about me and about life for this to be my new belief:

Saying "no"

Old thoughts/belief:

New thoughts/belief:

What I would need to know/see/feel was true about me and about life for this to be my new belief:

Contributing

Old thoughts/belief:

New thoughts/belief:

What I would need to know/see/feel was true about me and about life for this to be my new belief:

Being vulnerable

Old thoughts/belief:

New thoughts/belief:

What I would need to know/see/feel was true about me and about life for this to be my new belief:

Friends

Old thoughts/belief:

New thoughts/belief:

What I would need to know/see/feel was true about me and about life for this to be my new belief:

Honesty

Old thoughts/belief:

New thoughts/belief:

What I would need to know/see/feel was true about me and about life for this to be my new belief:

Intelligence

Old thoughts/belief:

New thoughts/belief:

What I would need to know/see/feel was true about me and about life for this to be my new belief:

I am clever

Old thoughts/belief:

New thoughts/belief:

What I would need to know/see/feel was true about me and about life for this to be my new belief:

I am worthy

Old thoughts/belief:

New thoughts/belief:

What I would need to know/see/feel was true about me and about life for this to be my new belief:

I am enough

Old thoughts/belief:

New thoughts/belief:

What I would need to know/see/feel was true about me and about life for this to be my new belief:

I am a meaningful part of the whole

Old thoughts/belief:

New thoughts/belief:

What I would need to know/see/feel was true about me and about life for this to be my new belief:

Well done today! Regardless of what came up for you, you're choosing to take new actions and this will always generate new results—each and every time. These results will accumulate into a very different reality, very soon, if not already.

I've been known to say and say and say again that self-realisation can be an ugly and messy process. You are brave and wonderful just for being on this journey of authentic personal empowerment! And you are strong and special for taking the time to actually do these exercises. There is no reaction without action so in taking the action you are causing new outcomes. This is something worth mentioning and celebrating many times during this book.

Day 10

Repetitive Patterns

There is no such thing as time inside your mind

What did you learn about yourself during the process in Day 9?

Very often there are recurring themes when answering the final question about what you'd need to know about yourself for the new belief to be true for you. These themes are also part of your guidance system for ongoing personal development.

Remember how you can't start speaking Russian without having some Russian data in your unconscious program? Well, here's some fantastic news for you:

The new thoughts and beliefs *you* choose are *only* possible because there *is* data in your unconscious *program* that has made them possible. So, as you've been able to imagine more positive thoughts, it means they're possible and you already have the raw ingredients you need.

Later on we will work with affirmations and also how to raise your energy to be in alignment with your new beliefs. You see, the better you feel, the easier it is to access more positive parts of your unconscious program, the worse you feel, the easier it is to access the worst thinking available in your unconscious program.

You have so much power to change your moment and; therefore, your life. It's an exciting journey to be on.

Today, with these repetitive patterns in mind, we are going to add a new element of understanding:

There is no such thing as time inside your mind.

It is possible to have a single experience that is so impactful it forever changes your perceptions in that context. As a child I loved and was fascinated with all animals. I would always befriend animals at new houses and look after any wildlife that got sick, or more often, injured themselves by flying full-speed into our tinted windows. When I was 11, I was delivering newspapers for my afternoon paper round and came across two large dogs, out on the street. I said, "Hello," in my normal friendly way and had my hand down for them to sniff so I could pat them and find their home, but instead they assumed an attack position and ran for me. I was so surprised that I didn't even defend myself. They got a couple of good bites into my legs before my screams roused neighbours and someone came out and dealt with it. I can't remember the details because I was in shock with all the bleeding and because I was so unaware that this kind of thing could happen to me. From this single experience, I created a strong fear of dogs. That one experience out-did the 11 years of positive experiences. I would be terrified of any dog off a leash, even the little ones. As an unprepared 11-year-old, I had few resources to protect myself in that situation. As a fit, healthy 25-year-old with 14 more years of life experience, my response to any dog off a leash was still exactly the same. I was bigger and stronger than the dogs that terrified me, but when a dog came along, mentally, I was 11 again.

Likewise, a scary experience in water as a child can create an adult that will not go in a pool or in the beach or a river. Often, it will create an adult that will not stand in water even up to their knees because they feel unsafe. It is the frightened child in them making that decision, not the fully resourced adult who is standing on safe, solid ground where there just happens to be water around.

I find this same adult-responding-like-a-child response when I work with clients on their long-term relationships. It shows up most often with family members. These otherwise intelligent, capable, and forthright human beings are unable to access these resources when confronted with a person or a situation that they experienced in their younger years, before they developed intelligence, capability and forthrightness.

Many years ago I worked with a high-level corporate executive called Jinny. She was referred to me by her naturopath to release work stressors. This intelligent, capable woman had a new boss and for unexplained reasons, her new work relationship was bringing up emotions and responses that she was not happy about. As we talked though the opening part of our session, she realised that her new boss was eliciting the same feelings she had experienced growing up with her mother. Due to the difference in contexts and radically different personalities of her boss and her mother, the similarity in her responses had not been obvious. As she described the relationship she'd had with her mother, it all became very clear. Whilst they shared a very loving, close relationship, she did say that the expectation was for her to contact her mother several times a day, all the way through her adult life since leaving home. She found this stifling, annoying and ridiculous, but was so affected by her mother's responses if she didn't call that she just 'did her duty' to avoid 'paying for it' later. Her mother was able to interpret many situations as, "I'm not important" or "Nobody cares about me." Jinny, a very intuitive woman was able to feel the intense expectations and emotional charge emanating from her mother and in the presence of that expectation felt powerless to express herself or take the kind of actions she would have liked to. Her mother passed away without Jinny ever expressing how those expectations made her feel or being able to recreate their relationship.

Jinny realised in the first session when it came to her mother's expectations, she'd respond like she did as a child. Her mother had a nervous breakdown when Jinny was nine and from that moment on she prioritised her mother's needs over her own and that pattern was never broken, even though consciously she had not made those links. When her mother would call her at work at 2 pm, after only speaking to Jinny in the morning, Jinny would feel the expectations and disappointments and respond like a nine-year-old in trouble.

Fast forward a few years and Jinny is presented with a new boss who also radiated intense emotionally-charged expectations. At the time, Jinny was in charge of a large team that she managed excellently and was also on the board of another organisation. She was not a woman lacking confidence or self-esteem and she had excellent communication skills, which is why her responses to this new boss surprised her. Jinny, now in her early 50's, and in the presence of the same type of communication as she had with her mother, she was responding, once again, like a nine-year-old in trouble.

These kinds of stories come from people of all ages and stages of life and the cure can be very simple. In just a few sessions, Jinny was able to totally recreate her relationship with her boss and respond in an empowered way using her current wisdom.

Talking to yourself is not the first sign of madness.

We all have conversations with ourselves in the privacy of our own minds. Although talking to yourself inside your head about how bad you look and how insufficient you are *is* a bit nutty, you can also use your ability to talk to yourself for the power of good. When you are in a situation where you are feeling out of sorts, ask yourself, "How old am I feeling?" If you feel that you're not behaving like your fully grown-up self then let your adult self, with the benefit of hindsight and all those extra years of life experience, talk to that younger you. Have an intentional conversation inside your mind, like a loving parent, talking with a younger child and be reassuring.

There is a massive difference in saying to yourself: a) *Oh my God, you idiot, I can't believe you're still nervous doing this stuff, imagine if they knew you felt like this, you'd lose your job you big faker!* and b) *It's alright . . . You're alright . . . It's OK to be nervous, this is a big presentation, but you know what? It's all going to be OK. You've done this many times and you're so brave for continuing to do it over and over again even though you're nervous. I'm proud of you! You're going to be just fine.*

If you're going to talk to yourself, then it may as well be loving and supportive—don't you think?

Today's Commitment to Authentic Personal Power

When you think about the patterns that revealed themselves to you on Days 8 and 9, how old do they feel?

Do you remember a time when they weren't with you?

As you go about your day, ask yourself: *How old do I feel?*

That's it, that's the commitment. Just keep asking. If you're happy or grumpy, bored or excited, just ask the question over and over throughout the day and see what comes up. I also want you to pay special attention to how your body feels.

The answer to the "How old do I feel?" question can come in many ways. It can be a number that pops into your head, something you see, hear or get a sense of or a picture of yourself at a certain age can come to you. All you need to do is ask the question and see what happens.

Before you continue with Day 11, take stock of your experiences with the last exercise.

Did you remain firmly in the 'now', feeling the resources of your current wisdom? If so, how did it feel inside your body? Did you feel light or heavy? Grounded or distant? What are the sensations of being in the now?

If you noticed different ages come up for you, how was that? What was it like in your body while you were connected to a younger, less experienced you?

Once you had that realisation, what difference did it make? Were you able to connect to your current self and respond differently?

Keep this tool up your sleeve forever more. It's always a good thing to understand yourself and your reactions. Sometimes the awareness itself is enough to snap you back in touch with your resources in the 'now'. Other times you may need to take your awareness off to someone who can specifically work with you, like I did with Jinny, to reroute your unconscious programming so you have access to all the great stuff in there.

DAY 11

Changing Your Mind

Change is totally safe.
You're more than good enough.
You can actually change anything you wish to

A first session with me will often involve a lot of sharing and deep, cathartic expression about how things are in the client's 'now'. It is very normal for me to be asked at some point during this process: "Do other people have these issues?"

The answer is for the most part 'no' with a bit of yes thrown in.

No, because we are all intricately unique. Even siblings growing up in the same environment will make different meanings from the same events and have different-looking 'now's.

And here's that little bit of yes: When boiled down to the very core, I have found that many issues come down to these common themes:

- I'm not good enough
  (and therefore there are others that are better and/or more deserving)
- There are some things you just can't change
  (so there's no point even trying)
  and
- Change isn't safe
  (Change involves letting go of certainty; therefore, change is scary and/or dangerous)

The tone of today, you might notice, will be a bit different and more direct. Your task is just to read through each section and perhaps, if it feels right, allow some perceptual changes to take place in your 'now'.

I'm not good enough—others are better and/or more deserving

If you've had these kinds of thoughts, I can totally relate. It's worth considering the possibility that it's not so much that you're not good enough—just that you're a work in progress. Just like me. You're on a journey; you're still growing and developing just like everybody else. Plus, keep in mind that just thinking something is true doesn't actually make it true. So the only thing that's true is that up until now you've had those kinds of thoughts about yourself. But that's a statement only about your thoughts, not about your real worth. And that doesn't mean that people who think differently are better or more deserving—it just means they think differently. Maybe they're more confident or maybe just more arrogant? And that's the real kicker that a lot of people don't stop to realise because arrogance doesn't make someone better or more deserving at all—in fact, it usually means just the opposite. It's a little like being a parent. Ask any good, loving parent if they've ever worried about whether they were doing a good job as a parent and, if they're being honest, they'll tell you that they've had those thoughts many times. That's one of the signs of a parent who truly cares about what's best for their child. Isn't that what being a good parent is all about?

So let's just stop for a second and think about what it takes to come up with a belief like, "I'm not good enough," in the first place. Somewhere, sometime, you started comparing yourself with somebody else. And if we're truly honest here, you probably started comparing your *idea* of yourself with your *idea* of that person. Nine times out of ten when people do that, it's a ludicrously unfair and distorted comparison. Just take a moment to think about how you've been doing that, and see for yourself . . .

It's important to take the time to realise when you're comparing someone else's highlight reel to your behind the scenes footage—there will be more to that person than meets your eye. This is the reason that I love the out-takes at the end of Jackie Chan movies—it reminds us that what appears seamless is actually the result of a whole lot of, sometimes painful, trial and correction.

So, regardless of whether or not comparing yourself to others is really worth doing, it's worth taking a moment to stop and ask yourself if you like the way it's been working out for you up until now—if not, maybe it's time to let that old way of thinking go now.

Especially since your attitude doesn't just affect you. I mean, did you ever stop to think about what message you've been sending to the people who look up to you by walking around in the world with those kinds of ideas in your head? Your friends? Your family? Your children?

Has buying into those thoughts shown them they can do whatever they put their heart and mind into, or has it shown them that they should give up on their dreams right from the start because there will always be someone better?

And besides . . . if that kind of belief ever actually had any substance to it, then how could you possibly be so arrogant as to think you're good enough to be the judge of who is and is not good enough? You simply wouldn't be qualified to make that kind of judgment about anyone—least of all about yourself! So stop being so judgmental and just get on with doing your thing already!

There are some things you just can't change, so there's no point even trying

This is a really interesting belief—and I could understand how you could think this if you had never experienced anything changing unexpectedly, but if you've ever experienced any kind of unexpected change then maybe you need to stop for a second and consider the possibility that maybe what you assume about what can and can't change isn't always necessarily how things really are.

And how can you really be sure about what can and can't change, anyway? Because frankly, if you've never personally done something, then you're probably the least qualified person to know if it's something that can be done.

And most of the time it's not so much the case that some things can't be changed, it's more that some things take more work to change. And for a lot of people, 'work' and 'hard' are four letter words. So sometimes it can be valuable to ask yourself whether this whole thing is about some things being impossible to change or it might just be something you tell yourself so you have an excuse to get out of having to work hard at things that take sustained effort. Because when something seems impossible to change, it's usually less about the thing itself and more about the fact that there are ways of thinking that can make change seem very difficult. So you have to ask yourself the question "Could the way I've been thinking be the very thing that's been making this seem impossible?"

And regardless of whether or not that's the case, the important thing is that you have been developing an awareness of what it is that you feel like you can't change—and without developing that awareness to begin with, nothing is likely to change in a hurry. So the fact that you're thinking that way now means that you've already made that first step towards making it possible for change to emerge over time. Because at the end of the day, there *are* some things you just can't change. Like the fact that things are going to change in life—and there's nothing you can do about that. So trying to hold on to a belief like this as if nothing's ever going to change is just a waste of energy, because there's no point trying to change the fact that things change in life. Because when you were six weeks old, you couldn't read—and nobody can change the fact that six week old babies generally can't read. But over time, things changed. And now here we are, and you're reading these very words. Check you out.

So let's say that a new political party comes into power with an overwhelming majority . . . and certain things that were once on the table subsequently get ruled out completely. That doesn't stop people thinking about how things could be different, does it? And that's a valuable process—because at some later stage that party may be voted out and a new one voted in, making possible what was previously impossible.

Because it's never that we can't do something—it's always that we can't do something *yet*. And *every single achievement in human history* started with someone trying to do something that had never been done before. Because it's not the things we *can* do, but the things we *can't* do—yet—that are worth pursuing the most.

So just look around at the fact that we can power things with electricity, fly through the sky to another country and see someone on the other side of the world while we're talking to them through a high speed internet connection. And now think of everyone who was ever involved in inventing the technology that allows us to do those things. Or just think about everyone who ever broke a world record. But think about those people, and just ask yourself what *they* would think about the idea that, 'there are some things you just can't change, so there's no point even trying.' Because if those people had bought into an idea like that, we wouldn't be living in the world we're living in right now.

So maybe it's not so much that there's no point trying to change things. Maybe it's just that there's no point continuing to think about things in a way that doesn't get you anywhere. Maybe it's just about finding and exploring a totally new approach that you had never thought about before . . . and continuing to do that until you discover yourself one day doing something that you thought was impossible before today.

Change isn't safe—Change involves letting go of certainty; therefore, change is scary and/or dangerous.

Ok, first of all: if this is a thought that resonates with you, and you're reading this right now, be careful—it's a slippery slope! After all, if you're reading something you've never read before, then you're doing something new—you're changing something. And who knows where this book might lead you? You're already exploring strange new territory just by reading this. Maybe you'll start entertaining all kinds of wild and unfamiliar ideas, and end up leaving your whole life behind—changing your name, your spiritual beliefs, your sexual preferences. Maybe you'll move to Uzbekistan, adopt a Welsh accent, and move into a yurt with two circus clowns and a dominatrix.

. . . or maybe none of that will happen. Maybe change is less about letting go of certainty and throwing yourself into some kind of chaotic maelstrom, and more about finally taking control and steering your life into clearer waters.

And who says things that involve uncertainty need to be scary or dangerous? Hell, watch a lawn bowls tournament some time. Anything could happen on the day. One player might be in the zone, another might make a couple of stupid mistakes. But scary? Hardly. Dangerous? Hell no. I mean, if you parachute off skyscrapers for fun and you pack your parachute in a totally new way that nobody has ever done before, then I can imagine how that could be scary and potentially very dangerous indeed. In that kind of situation, letting go of certainty might well be a dangerous thing to do. But in lawn bowls—and most other things in life—uncertainty very, very rarely involves anything genuinely dangerous.

I mean think about the fact that you're reading this right now. There was a time in your life when you couldn't read. You didn't know how. And at some point you started to learn. And you didn't know for sure when you first started to learn if it was going to be easy or hard, whether you'd be a good reader or if you'd struggle. And yet here we are. The world didn't end. Life went on. And not only did life go on, but you learned many things in that time. You've probably read a few things in your life that made you smile. Maybe you even read some things that made you laugh.

And laughter often comes from uncertainty. We laugh at things that delight us unexpectedly. Watch children—they do this all the time! And they play games, which *always* have some element of uncertainty. That's what makes them fun! In games, complete predictability is boring. Kids experience joy in shaping the way a game plays out. And everyone was a kid once—even you.

Plus, on a more serious note: clinging to the belief that change is scary and dangerous . . . in a world where stuff inevitably happens, things inevitably change around us, and we need to adapt . . . is a very dangerous thing to do. It can turn you into a bunny in the headlights, and that's not good at all.

Besides, it's usually the *thought* that's scary, rather than the thing itself. You probably already know this. It's just like when something small casts a big shadow because of the direction of the light. So it's usually not so much that change itself is scary, but rather that you happen to be really good at scaring yourself with the way you *think* about change. So when you think about the way you have thought about this kind of thing up until now, what do you do inside your mind? Do you think about all the ways things could go wrong, or all the ways things could go right? Do you think about small, modifiable changes, or do you only think about massive 'no going back' kind of changes? And when you think about the way you've been thinking about these things, has that way of thinking been serving you well and supporting and sustaining exactly the kind of life you want to live, or have you just been keeping yourself stuck in a life you can tolerate? Because ultimately, it's not about whether or not the idea of uncertainty is something you can get scared about—it's about whether or not you're living a life that you love.

Today's Commitment to Authentic Personal Power

List three reasons why are you totally and completely worthy and good enough to pursue and achieve your goals:

1)

2)

3)

Ponder the results of achieving those goals and all the positive outcomes that will occur in your life as a direct result. List three changes that you are now thoroughly looking forward to experiencing:

1)

2)

3)

DAY 12

Changing You = Changing the World Part 1

How you can positively impact those around you, for everyone's benefit

**The only person you can change
is yourself, and when you change
yourself,**

**the whole world around you reflects
that transformation.**

Have you come across this as a theory before, that when you change; the world changes around you? What has your response to it been? How do you feel reading it now?

I work with clients all the time who, when they begin, are convinced that the people in their outside world are unchangeable. They believe the behaviour of others is set, and this is just the way it's going to be. These people are at *effect*.

A relationship is a *nominalisation* (the use of a verb or an adjective as a noun). We talk about the relationship, our relationship, and their relationship as if it's a noun, a real thing, and it's not. The relating part of relationship is something we do; it's a verb. We relate to one another. Sometimes we relate to certain people more than others.

How are you choosing to relate to the people in your life?

Every single day you create the quality of your relationships by how and if you choose to relate to the people in your life. In a two-person scenario, you have 50% of the power to sway how the relationship will go and 100% power on how *you* choose to be and if *you* choose to continue relating with the person/people in the relationship.

I worked with a client once, who was convinced that her husband's family hated her and wanted her life to go badly. In her first session, she told me all about how they didn't include her in anything and then talked about all the things that happened in her absence (on purpose, so she'd know that she was really excluded). She 'knew' that she just wasn't in the family 'click'. She told me they were the kind of family that got together at least once a week, which was far too often in her opinion. Because she felt so uncomfortable, she avoided as many of those get togethers as possible and ideally would only visit once a month. She also told me they were the kind of family that all knew each other's business, and when you visited, they'd tell you all about what was going on in everybody's lives that weren't there at the event. This horrified her because she was extremely private and didn't ever want any of her personal business being discussed when she wasn't around, so she chose to never share anything personal and kept her relationships with her husband's family very surface-level-only.

Can you see what's actually going on here?

She chose to keep her relating to surface-level niceties and then felt rejected that the relationships she had with her husband's family were surface-level-only. She chose to avoid family get togethers whenever possible and then felt excluded when the events she missed were being discussed. She also chose to never get involved in conversations about other people's news because she felt like it was a violation of their privacy.

So what was she actually doing when she was with her husband's family?

She never asked anything personal because she didn't want to seem nosey. She gave very little information about herself because she felt others were being nosey. She sat in silence while conversation went on around her and then felt excluded and uncomfortable.

Living life at *cause* means knowing that in every scenario, there is always choice. In this example above, assuming that this client valued her husband's feelings and desires for her to share in his close family ties the, "I choose to have nothing to do with any of them," option isn't really an option she'd like to choose. Let's be honest here, most of us have people in our lives that we need to have relationships with who wouldn't personally be our first choice. Being willing to adjust your behaviour and being flexible will enhance these relationships enormously. Ask yourself, what does this other person need?

I had someone in my life for many years, the mother of someone extremely dear to me, who suffered with terribly low self-esteem and who was constantly asking for positive feedback.

For this woman, one thank you or one compliment was never enough; she'd come right back at you two minutes later and ask for some more, "Do you really like my curtains?" Initially I interpreted this as a very frustrating neediness. My time in that family's home was annoying, and I used to point out that I'd already told her how much I liked the curtains. Then, I got flexible, and decided to take charge of my relating. So, I would be complimentary about everything I saw for the first five minutes of my visits and gave at least three or four different compliments every time she did anything or cooked anything, grew anything, wore anything—you get the idea. I took charge with some upfront behaviour that transformed every visit from then on. I gave her what she needed right up front, and she never said anything needy ever again. In fact, her stories, her relating to me and everyone else in the room became about positive things (not stories where she needed the people in the room to tell her how appreciated and valuable she was). If it ever slipped back into needy stories, I took that as my feedback that I needed to revert to the upfront compliments and in one visit, it would all be sorted. I wanted to feel comfortable while I was there and I was 100% responsible for that, so I took charge. This person outside of me; who others saw as static and unchangeable, changed into someone that I genuinely enjoyed the company of because I was flexible enough to meet her needs upfront, for my own comfort. Let me also be very clear that all my compliments were about things that I genuinely liked. I am a woefully inept liar and could never tell someone I liked their new curtains if I didn't (because it would be totally obvious that I was making it up).

For the client who had fixed ideas about her husband's family, she needed to get into *cause* with her relationships there and make some new choices. We worked together on areas of her life she was happy to share with them. The areas she chose were work, and her personal development journey (what she was learning rather than the details of her personal transformation). Once she was willing to share, her husband's family felt like she'd opened up and like she was part of the family, where previously they felt like she didn't want to be there (and they were right). She felt more comfortable and attended more family gatherings. When the family would discuss previous memories, she joined in rather than sitting on the sidelines. By being in charge of yourself and making upfront changes, the people around you will respond differently.

Now, if what your in-laws want is for you to think it's wonderful for their gargantuan slobbery dog to lick you on the face (because that's how he lets you know that he lurrrves you), and you're more of a mutual-consent person in the licking department; your upfront flexibility doesn't have to be putting up with doggy slobber all over your cheek and lips and pretending you love it. You do; however, have a multitude of choices in how to deal with and resolve reoccurring issues when you understand that you are at *cause*. In this situation, I would ask myself, what do these people need to feel respected and like you 'get' them? There will be other things you can do that will more than make-up for not wanting to be pashed by the dog.

When you take charge of how you choose to relate, it will change your relationships. In the past, you may have forgotten that we can actually choose to leave relationships. In the past, you may not have realised that *you* have the power to relate differently. When you choose to relate differently and still get really unpleasant results; you get to make new choices. To stay, to go, to accept the person as they are and stay off the topics where your values are wildly different, to stop giving the level of information that can then hurt you, to see them less . . . so many options and you get to choose them all. You can't feel trapped in something that you chose. Just being at cause will energetically shift things for the better. So be brave and try new things.

No one outside of you is EVER to blame for what you have inside you.

Today's Commitment to Authentic Personal Power

Pick one person and one of their behaviours that seem set-in-stone and that really bugs you.

Ask yourself: When this behaviour is happening, what is this person actually needing from me?

Am I providing what they need when I respond in my usual manner?

Am I willing to provide what they need?

If not, why not? What might happen if I provide what they need?

What are some of the things I could try doing differently to generate a different result?

Commit to trying those things you could do differently in your future interactions with that person. You may be extremely surprised by the results!

DAY 13

Affirmations

How to make them actually work

Why practise affirmations?

How can I use them effectively?

What can affirmations do for me and what are their limitations?

If you look up *affirmations* in the dictionary, there are several meanings. In the context of this book, *affirmations* refer to saying positive stuff to yourself, on purpose, to create positive change in your life.

Our unconscious mind doesn't actually know the difference between what's real and what's imagined. That's why you can imagine something awful and burst into tears when nothing is actually happening. Or why when someone talks about a spider, you can get all creepy and crawly somewhere on your body. The great thing about that is using it, on purpose, to make new experiences seem not-so-new. What your mind feels like it's done 100 times before is not going to be as hard to do as something that feels totally new.

Remember back to Day 2—Your Thoughts Generate Your Feelings . . . whether you're doing it on purpose, or not, your mind can run wild and make wild feelings happen. How you feel is going to determine how you act and the results you are creating in your life. So, it makes sense to want to direct your mind on to thinking about positive, fun, heart-warming stuff, doesn't it? When you think positive thoughts, how much better do you feel?

Worrying is like praying for what you don't want

When I was introduced to using affirmations as a discipline, it was in a spiritual context. I was taught that, by using Universal Laws, my thoughts were able to attract into my life the experiences I wished to have. We haven't yet arrived to the part of our 42-day journey that will explore your energetic vibration and its influence in creating your life, but even once we have, all that is said today still holds true.

Why use affirmations?

There are several positive reasons to choose to say affirmations throughout your day:

1) The thought itself will create positive feelings and make you feel good right now.
2) The practice of focusing your mind on positive thinking will strengthen the habit of thinking positively more often (even when you're not doing your affirmations).
3) It is something you can very easily choose to do because it requires no external help or equipment—you always have your mind with you! Every single time you choose to take action to feel better, it strengthens the deep, inner knowing that you are in charge of your life . . . no one else . . . just beautiful You.

There has been a lot of research completed on the mind and body connection. We know, scientifically that thoughts have physiological effects. In sports institutes the world over, top athletes are using the power of their minds to visualise their events positively, with well-documented, positive results. I watched a television show once showing that gymnasts who mentally rehearsed a new trick were more successful when doing it physically the first time than those who did not. The Llewellyn Encyclopedia shares that visualisation "increases confidence and motivation" in athletes and also "sharpens players muscles." *http://www.llewellyn. com/encyclopedia/article/244).*

If you want to have a new experience in life, creating an affirmation and working with it every day will increase the likelihood of you having that experience (even without taking into account that we live in a vibrational universe).

How to practise affirmations:

You can create affirmations about anything you like. They can be focused on feeling a particular way or experiencing a particular thing. They can be general, they can be specific—it's really up to you. As long as you follow the guidelines, they will be doing you good.

There are actually several guidelines to follow when creating affirmations for yourself—if you want them to be useful!.

1) The statement has to be positive.

So often, when we are thinking about what we want to create in our lives, we are thinking about the lack of that thing. I want to feel less tired. I want to be less stressed—the focus is on tired and stressed, rather than on energised and relaxed.

Here's what NOT to do:
I'm so happy that I'm not single anymore.
I'm not scared anymore of being judged for being fat.
Here's an example of what to do instead for the same outcome:
I'm so happy in my relationship.
I love the security and acceptance I feel each and every day.

2) When you say the affirmation it makes you feel GREAT!

This will most often relate to how much you believe the statement. For example, if I (a non-gymnast) was imagining doing the triple-spiked-hoopla-ha and saying an affirmation about how ace I am at it, I would believe it less than someone who can already do the double-spiked-hoopla-ha. That said we normally want to stretch ourselves with affirmations, so the trick is to not stretch *too* far.

If I want to run a 40km marathon, but right now I only get off the couch to go to the toilet (and I get really puffed walking those 15 steps) then, "I felt so great winning the New York marathon," might be too much of a stretch and actually make me drop into some negative self-talk. That negative self talk might drop me into memories of not achieving previous goals which can make me feel revolting (and them I'm going to have to have a bar of chocolate to cheer me up, and the cycle continues!). Just like we break down goals, it's a good exercise to break down affirmations, too. The sweet spot is for your affirmation to excite you and generate positive feelings, but not stretch too far and become something your mind cannot grasp you actually doing. What is "too far" is a very individual thing. Some people are extremely good at setting huge goals and just knowing they'll get there (and never get down about how long it's taking). Other people are much better at enjoying incremental successes. You will know the sweet spot for you based on how your affirmation makes you feel. If it feels yuck or completely unbelievable; STOP, and go back a step and then see how that feels. Always choose affirmations that make you feel great because when you feel great you respond differently to the outside world. When you are acting and reacting, like the person you want to be, whatever your affirmation is about, then you're more likely to create the right circumstances to make it happen. Choosing to feel great, right now, is the best way to create a better "right now."

3) The statement is in the present or past tense (not future tense).

For example, if your affirmation was, "I *will* totally love living in my new house" what you're actually affirming is not having a new house now. Instead it would be better for your affirmation to be, "I totally love *living* in my new house" or "The day I moved into my new house was one of the happiest of my life." In these statements, there is no longing for the new house—you're already in it.

We want your brain to imagine already having the thing or experience. You can also take your mind out into the future with your affirmation, so it's a statement of remembering back to when it was exciting and new to have the thing. For example, "I was amazed that it only took a few months of living in my dream home for me to stop being WOWed every morning and for it to just feel like home."

4) You can make a picture of it inside your head.

Some people are naturally very talented at visualising and others aren't, but every person has an imagination. When you're making pictures inside your head, you are still totally seeing what's going on outside of you, it's not that you have to see something like a virtual tour that looks so real you could reach out and touch it. Take a moment to think about a telephone . . . you made a picture in your head, yes? Was it a mobile phone, a home phone, a public phone booth? You can answer the question because you made a picture. If you struggle with making pictures, then look up. It is easier to make pictures when you eyeballs are looking up (I won't go into the science of it, just trust me!).

So, make a picture of your affirmation being realised. If your affirmation is something like, "I'm fit and healthy and I love my life," then ask yourself: "What will I be doing when I'm living that reality?" And then make a picture yourself doing those activities.

You don't have to visualize your affirmation every time you say it. What's important is that you can have pictures that go with the affirmation. It makes it easier for your brain to feel like it's common territory, just like that triple-spiked-hoopla-ha that's being perfected somewhere in the world right now.

These are the basic guidelines for using affirmations. They can be as long or as short as you like. If you're a precise and to-the-point person then your affirmations should be, too. If you're more flowery and extravagant in your language, then your affirmations should be too. Make them your own.

Here's one more tip: Try singing your affirmations. You know how easy it is to get a catchy tune stuck in your head, right? Well, pick a catchy tune, and make the words of your affirmation fit that tune. That way you'll find yourself accidentally thinking positively while having a song you like running on your internal sound system. I've spent so many years doing this and it really improves how I feel when doing my affirmations. For me it was the missing ingredient. Music will uplift your mood and change your feelings. Add positive lyrics to that and hey presto . . . magic happens inside your being. When I opened my first clinic, I took a football team's club anthem and used that tune to sing, "I am fully booked, each day I work" and a whole lot of other lines about having an abundant business. If you want to see this idea in action, (minus the football theme) go and check out *www.singyouraffirmations.com.au*. I released a CD back in 2009 of affirmations to music and I continue to get great feedback from people who listen and sing-a-long (inside their heads or out loud) while they are going about their day. Unlike quiet, meditative affirmation CDs; this one has music and singing so you can listen while you walk or clean the house or do other every day activities. I strongly suggest singing your affirmations—try it and see what happens for yourself.

What affirmations can do and what their limitations are.

Affirmations allow you to tap into the positive resources of your unconscious mind. They put you in a place of creative power and smooth the pathway to practical, physical change. The most important thing they do is make you feel good, right now, and right now in the moment that you're in, choosing new actions and generating new results. The limitations come if you are ever doing an affirmation that violates your unconscious values or that doesn't feel safe for some part of you. It's a silly example, I know, but no amount of affirmations could make you feel safe enough to put your hand in a blender (please don't try this at home!). Affirmations that violate your values or are unsafe in any way generally don't feel great when you do them (see guideline number two). Just be aware that you have an unconscious program and sometimes one-on-one individual help is needed to achieve lifelong transformations. To put this into context, let me give you a more sensible example than the blender. I've worked with many people over the years that have deep-seated unconscious fear of receiving help or being reliant on any person other than themselves. This comes about for a variety of reasons and takes time and support to change (if the person ever wants to). If someone was unaware of this, at the conscious level, and doing an affirmation like, "Every day I receive emotional and financial support," there would be unconscious resistance to taking on the new belief. I'm explaining this because if your affirmations aren't working for you, this may be something you want to look into.

Today's Commitment to Authentic Personal Power

Craft yourself an affirmation that follows the guidelines set out today.

Five times, over the next 24 hours, complete the following exercise:

Spend one minute saying your affirmation, over and over, making pictures of it being real and happening in your life. Let the feelings that come from thinking in this new way, uplift you right now and smile.

Done.

Before moving on, make some notes:

What is your affirmation?

What are the pictures that go with it?

Did it change throughout the day?

Could you commit to continuing this practice?

If yes, fantastic, if no, what can you choose to commit to? Even doing something for one or two minutes a day has a huge effect on your unconscious mind.

Every day that you choose to take new actions you are generating new results. Take a moment to congratulate yourself, for being the awesome being that you truly are!

Day 14

Guilt

Understanding it and letting it go

I have stated earlier in our journey that, in my opinion, there is no such thing as a negative emotion. Our feelings are there as part of our life experience and to guide us to take action. I am quite happy to say though that guilt is the most useless emotion of all to bother holding on to . . . and I'll explain why.

What would it be like if all the guilt you've ever felt disappeared out of your body and mind? Would it be OK with your unconscious mind if that were to happen? If you think that holding on to guilt is actually a good thing, then prepare to be challenged on that. If you'd love to let your guilt go, but don't know how to, then prepare for a doorway to freedom to be opened within yourself.

There are two different kinds of guilt:

1) I have said/done/thought something that went against my own values.
2) I have said/done/thought something that went against the values of *so-and-so-important-person-that-I-want-to-love-and-approve-of-me*.

These are two very different things so let's look at them separately:

1) We are very diverse people here on planet Earth and our values are, likewise, diverse. To quote myself, "There's no such thing as right or wrong, it's all just perception." (*Love's Alive—Positively Funky Affirmations for Anybody, Anytime & Anywhere*). This first kind of guilt is what you feel when you have violated your own values. For example, you may value the honour of your 'word' and you've promised not to share some private, personal information. Then in a moment of enjoying the attention you're getting or an angry, pained "stuff you!" kind of a moment, you break your word and share something you know you shouldn't have. You've violated your own ideals, you feel terrible and we label these horrible feelings as 'guilt'.

2) The second kind of guilt is more to do with your unconscious mind's program. In this instance, you do something that your adult self thinks is acceptable, but the guilt begins when you think about *so-and-so-important-person-that-I-want-to-love-and-approve-of-me* and how horrified they'd be by what you just did/said/thought.

With regards to the first type of guilt described above, let me tell you a little story:

When I was four, my mother smoked cigarettes. She used to light them in the car with this little push-in lighter. One day, while I was in the car and she wasn't, I pushed in the lighter, took it out and looked at the pretty orange light inside. I touched the pretty orange light . . . and burned my finger quite badly. In my line of work, we call this a 'single-trial learning'. One experience that taught me to never, ever again touch the pretty orange light of the car-cigarette-lighter because it really, *really* hurt! As is the way with our magical, self-healing bodies, my body's wellness system produced a blister and within a few weeks my finger was back to its normal self without even a scar to remind me of the experience. What do you think happened to my 'single-trial learning'? Once the blister went away, do you think I went back and tried it again? Did my unconscious mind need to keep the blister there, hurting me every day, to remind me not to retry the finger-on-car-lighter trick? No. So, why do you think you choose to hold on to old guilt? What have you learned from the old experiences that you are still choosing to feel guilty about?

Or more to the point, what haven't you learned?

As a four-year-old, I chose to learn: Never do that again, it hurt! Can you choose the same thing right now with regards to whatever you're choosing to still feel guilty about? When you choose to have a powerful learning experience, that learning can remain with you, ALWAYS, but you can allow the blister of painful guilt to heal itself, right now. Does that make sense? Sometimes, all you need is the learning and the guilt is no longer necessary. Other times, with this kind of guilt, there's action to take, to make things right again. So, ask yourself: What is the right thing to do now? If you violated your values by sharing information you shouldn't have, do you need to tell the person whose trust you've violated and sincerely apologise?

I often work with clients who are holding on to guilt to ensure they don't do the same thing again. In my experience, if you're still feeling guilty, it's probably because you wouldn't mind doing the same thing again (see guilt type 2) or, you're into the idea that punishing yourself is a good thing. My question to you then would be: how long do you want to keep punishing yourself for? What goodness are you creating in the world by keeping yourself feeling awful?

What are you avoiding in your life by making sure that you keep that old guilt alive? Have a look around at the people you admire . . . are they the ones who feel the guiltiest or the people who are doing admirable things? Guilt isn't admirable, but action can be. So, take the actions set out in today's Commitment to Authentic Personal Power below and choose the freedom to admire yourself and your actions.

Now, let's move on to the second type of guilt. In life, we learn all our valuable skills through trial and correction. In the first type of guilt, we try something, we don't like it (or how it makes us feel) so we correct, make amends if necessary and do something different. Problem solved. With this other type of guilt, you're more than likely going to keep ploughing on doing the thing that you're also spending time feeling guilty about. You trialled it and you liked it, so there might not be a whole lot of correcting going on. So, your values are conflicted. Part of you wants to keep on doing the thing, and part of you sits in judgment of yourself. Does this make sense?

What's required are some effective questions. Read the two sets of questions below and answer the set that you relate to most.

Today's Commitment to Authentic Personal Power

Guilt Type 1: I have said/done/thought something that went against my own values.

If guilt of the first kind is an issue for you then make a list of all the things you feel guilty about and answer these questions:

I feel guilty about:

What is the one thing I could decide right now, that would show me that I've learned what I need to learn about this experience?

What action do I need to take to make this right for myself?

What action, if any, do I need to take to make this right for anyone else involved?

With this learning and action completed, what new thoughts can I have about myself and about my life?

Taking into account how much time I used to spend thinking those old thoughts and how much time I can now spend with my new thoughts (that were possible because of my learning and action), what new feelings will I feel?

Immerse yourself now in imagining those new feelings . . . what new actions will you take as an immediate result of feeling that new way?

When you've finished reading this sentence, shut your eyes for a moment, and imagine your life six months from now . . . all those new thoughts, the actions you took, those new feelings and new actions that you've been experiencing . . . think of all the flow-on benefits from the changes you decided to make . . . go there now and imagine . . . and when you get back, write down the three most significant changes that happened as a direct result of your choice to release guilt today:

1)

2)

3)

Go through this process with everything on your list of things you feel guilty about. Or not. The choice is always yours, but if you want to experience some new results, then you need to take new actions.

Guilt Type 2: I have said/done/thought something that went against the values of so-and-so-important-person-that-I-want-to-love-and-approve-of-me.

If the second kind of guilt is an issue in your life, then please make a list of all the things you feel guilty about. Then ask yourself the questions below and write down your answers. Just like on yourself assessment day, it's really important to write down the very first thing that comes to your mind. You may even write down something you weren't expecting on the list of things you feel guilty about. You may notice that partway through the questions, the idea that you need to feel guilty about that thing just goes away and you feel free to behave in accordance with your own present-day values. You may notice it more at the end of the questions that your perception has shifted. It's also very common that a couple of weeks after doing this process, you find yourself with new thoughts and feelings about that old thing you used to feel guilty about. Sometimes you don't even notice until months later, when someone else is talking about feeling guilty, that you just haven't felt that way for AGES.

I feel guilt about doing/saying/being:

How old was I when I decided that this was 'wrong'?

Was it my idea or someone else's idea?

If it was your idea, then go on an imaginary journey back to the moment in time that you were making sense of the world outside of you and came up with the understanding that this thing was wrong. It's OK to feel that this is make believe, and allow your unconscious mind (the part that creates your dreams that doesn't always make sense) to create a scenario you can look at. It's also OK if you can actually remember the event itself. Go there now—watching that scenario, understand now that the younger version of you is making meaning from those events. If you were to re-experience that event, but as an adult, with the benefit of hindsight and all the wisdom that you now have, what would be your new interpretation of the event?

What new meaning would you make, knowing everything you now know?

Now that you have a new perspective, how easy is it to be totally comfortable with doing that thing that you used to feel guilty about?

If it was someone else's view then ask yourself this:

Whose idea is was it that this action is wrong/bad?

Is that person right about absolutely everything they believe to be true?

How many other things do you have different values about?

If they like vanilla ice-cream and you like peppermint choc-chip, would that be OK?

What is it that makes this different?

If they never understood or respected that you had a different set of thoughts, about this thing (or even about the ice-cream) could that be OK?

Would you be giving them information about the benefits of peppermint choc-chip and try and get them to like it too, or at least celebrate your right to choose your own flavour, or would you just be able to quietly, inside your mind, agree to disagree?

What would you need to know about yourself and about your right to choose your life to be totally comfortable with having different opinions on things with this person?

What do you make it mean that this person doesn't value your choice of action or that they wouldn't if they knew what you've been up to?

What else could you make it mean instead?

What positive benefit or need has there been to holding on to this guilt?

What do you need to learn to meet that need in a new, empowering way?

How is letting that old guilt go going to change your life?

How is releasing the guilt you were holding on to going to improve the relationship you have with you?

How is releasing the guilt you were holding on to going to improve the other relationships you have?

What new feelings can you then have about yourself and about life?

And what new actions can you take as a direct result?

How do you feel right now?

Make a note in your calendar/diary/smart *thing* for 3 months from today's date to come back to this exercise and see just how far you've come since letting that old guilt go.

Day 15

Shifting Perceptions

How to walk a mental-mile in anyone's
shoes and choose the most useful perspective

Most of us have heard the proverb that we shouldn't judge someone until we've walked a mile in their shoes. How often do you put that into practice? Today we're going to learn how to do just that (minus walking the mile and shoes actually being required).

Today I am calling you forth to trust your unconscious mind and be willing to do something that will be quite new for most of you. For this exercise I'm going to teach you to make sense, I'm going to have to do some explaining before we get started. So here it goes:

Your unconscious mind has been collecting data since your time in the womb. Thankfully, we have a conscious interface so we don't have to be consciously aware of everything we've ever seen, heard, smelt, felt, tasted and sensed for our entire existence (imagine all that mental noise!!). So, like a huge, ancient library, you have countless bits of data about human beings in general from all the conversations you've had with people, about themselves and about other people they know plus the television shows you've watched, books you've read and conversations with people about the television and books they've seen . . . you get the idea—there's a LOT of information in that mind of yours. Imagine how much your unconscious mind has absorbed about the people closest to you. There is so much going on during your interactions with people that are outside your conscious awareness, but being fully recorded and stored by your unconscious mind. You can choose to use this information for a much greater understanding of yourself and the people around you.

Expanded perception exercise

1) Decide on a relationship or interaction that you'd like to improve

For now, while you are learning to use this technique, please choose an interaction that only has one person other than you. As you get more skilled in using this tool, you can practice with a presentation at work or a whole-family get together and see what everyone is experiencing, but like anything, start simply, and get the skills, then expand upon them when you choose to.

2) Engage a playful state of mind.

It is possible to do deep and transformational personal development work with a light heart and playful attitude. If at any point during this exercise you find yourself trying to get it perfectly correct then just stop and come back to it later when you can be supported by another person or when you are just in a more adventurous, anything-goes kind of mood.

Think about how you normally interact with this person. Is it standing up or sitting down?

3) Set three places on the floor with chairs or pieces of paper on the ground.

The first two places represent you and the other person and should be a similar distance apart to how you would be regularly communicating. If you interact in a variety of ways, just make it a distance that you would be comfortable with under normal circumstances.

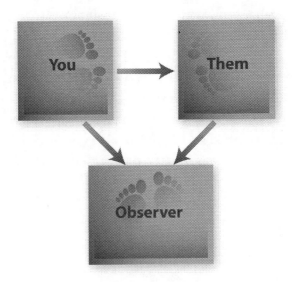

The third space is an observer position and should be an equal distance from both other positions and far enough away that it feels like the observer could have a good look at the two people without being involved at all.

For the purpose of explaining clearly, I am going to imagine that you're standing. Just make the necessary adjustments if you'll be sitting down.

4)   Step into the 'You' space and imagine interacting with this person.

Stand how you would normally stand in such an interaction. You should think of how you feel, how you breathe, your posture and body language. Think of an interaction with this person and imagine yourself in it—life size and happening now like you've stepped into a virtual reality simulation. So you're inside 'you' and looking through your own eyes, out at this person. If you need to close your eyes to bring up the feelings you normally feel then do.

Take special notice of how big or small you feel and what comes up in your body and mind.

If some conversations with this person are easy and others are hard and you wish you could be more resourced within them, then choose to imagine the latter. If you notice size differences (e.g. you're smaller or bigger or they are) then even that up so that it is a correct representation of physical reality.

Being you, imagine the interaction unfolding, see their responses, imagine what they say back and their tone and body language. Let the interaction unfold and notice it all. You may also be more aware of all the meanings you're making about their words, facial expressions and posture.

5)   Step into the 'Observer' space and replay the interaction.

Watch those two people over there interacting with each other. You've been watching other people your whole life so this is nothing new. As a neutral and indifferent observer ask yourself questions like: I wonder how these people know each other; what is the relationship between those people like? Does one or both of them look stressed or relaxed, emotionally engaged or disinterested? If you could see the energy between them as moving colours what would that be like? Do they both want to be there? And any other questions that come to your mind as an observer to their interaction.

Now, move as far away from your chairs or pieces of paper as you can (while still seeing them) . . .

6) Imagine that you are an alien scientist, here from a different galaxy in a hidden research pod and you are watching this interaction. It is your first ever human observation and you have no idea what the culture here is like and who these people are to each other. Step into your curious, scientific mind and ask yourself questions like: What are the customs of this world? Is this a peaceful and harmonious place? Is one of these human beings the leader of the other? Is this a mating ritual?

If the alien had equipment to measure and observe the mental and emotional frequency of the interaction, what would the results be? And what might the alien make those results mean?

7) Step into the 'Them' space and replay the interaction again.

It's very important that you quite literally step into being the other person. Again, like it's virtual reality and this time you're playing the other role and are the viewer inside the other person's experience. Adopt the same physiology—stand like they would, breathe like they would, have the same gestures and facial expressions.

Looking through their eyes, watch the character that is you, standing how you stand, gesturing how you do, watch the face and the body language.

How does it feel? How is this person interpreting the behaviour of you over there? What meanings are they making while watching you and experiencing this interaction?

8) Step back into the 'Observer' space one more time.

Has anything changed? What can you notice now between those two people?

9) Come back to the 'You' space with all that you've learned and your expanded perspectives in place.

The first time I did this exercise, I chose an interaction with a dear friend from my childhood. We were very close, but I was always a bit guarded and kept parts of my thoughts and activities from her because I feared she would be judgmental and openly critical. I had been convinced of how she "saw" me, and my behaviour reflected that. I was quite certain through my 20s that she felt that she was "better" than me, smarter and more "ahead" in life. When I did this exercise I realised I was looking up to her, quite literally, even though in our adult form I am several inches taller. When I mentally allowed myself to become life-size, instead of miniature, I felt more present in the now and stopped accessing my childhood uncertainty. As I stepped into being her and looking at myself though her eyes I experienced how she saw me in a completely different way. I felt the love and admiration she had for me. I felt the rejection that my guarded behaviour caused her. I experienced her lack of awareness of what was going on for me. It was relationship changing! Whether my new perception was an accurate mind-read is really not important because it transformed the way that I behaved in that relationship and that change resulted in a deeper connection and more heartfelt, honest interaction. In the past there had been subservience and this exercise corrected that. The relationship now reflects that change as we both feel a mutual respect and we communicate from a place where there are rarely the misunderstandings that were prevalent before. And, if there is a misunderstanding then we can talk about it easily and it's resolved without angst.

Today's Commitment to Authentic Personal Power

Choose a relationship that really matters to you and try the exercise outlined today. Make sure you spend enough time in each position to really get a feeling for how each person is experiencing the interaction. Make any corrections you need to with sizing. Follow all the steps and when you're done, answer these questions:

What did you see, hear and feel while 'inside' the other person?

How were they feeling?

How did they perceive you?

Was it different to what you previously thought?

How can you apply this new perception in your next interaction?

Can you see other relationships benefiting from you now having this tool in your tool kit for Authentic Personal Power?

DAY 16

Blurk—feeling down, dark and unmotivated

Understanding why you go there and how to get out

Blurk is a term I use to describe that place of *slumpy* heaviness when everything feels like a burden and difficult to do, you're grumpy, you have a short fuse and the things that used to feel light and fun just seem like too much effort. Do you know the place I mean?

Over my years of studying in spiritual groups, I've come up against what I've been taught to think of as my 'Ego': a part of me, that was wholeheartedly against me evolving and becoming a limitless, shining light of awesomeness (to borrow a word from Kung Fu Panda). I learned that when I made a commitment and the voice inside my head said, "No, stay in bed," I was to treat it mean and plough on regardless. I was taught that my mission in life was to win and beat this Ego so that I could stand strong and be in control of my life.

I've since learned that starting up arguments inside one's own mind can cause problems as well as solve them. As I've said before, talking to yourself is not a sign of madness, in fact we all do it, but it doesn't mean that arguing is useful. I now have a new belief and way of dealing with the negative, fearful or unmotivated thoughts that work against the realisation of people's goals and dreams.

Remember back to all the talk we've been doing about your *program*. Most of it was set in place by the time you were seven years old. What was life like for you in those years from birth to seven? Do you remember much of it? Whether we had the fairy tale, happy-parents upbringing or something horrific, there were times for all of us in childhood where we learned, "Don't" and "Shouldn't" and "You can't do that." When a little person hears that they can't do something, they generally don't have the adult wisdom to see it from the adult's perspective. Heck, most of us as adults can find it hard sometimes to see things from another's point of view. So, that "little you" was a meaning-maker, just like "big you" is, and whether it was directly said, or interpreted, "little you" got the ideas about how things are, established a self-image and worked out what got attention and what didn't. This "little you" learned how to exist in the world from these interactions and came up with some frameworks that might still be alive today. Things like, "I'm not good enough/funny enough/smart enough/loved enough" or "If I can't do it perfectly the first time then I shouldn't even try because people will laugh at me."

When young people are reprimanded, they make meanings from that. When young people are excluded, they make it mean things. When young people are left alone or with people they'd rather not be with, they make that mean things. When young people can't physically do something they see older people doing, they make meanings from that, too.

These notions are often the main messages of the Ego. So, when I come across these voices in myself or with clients, the first thing I do is take the limiting belief or unpleasant emotion and honour and respect it enough to find out why it's there. Your unconscious mind doesn't hold on to things without a positive intention.

Let me give you some examples of this for you to see the pattern:

Doreen came to see me after having a stroke. She was in her late 20s, and feeling totally *blurk* about pretty much every aspect of her life. After many sessions, as she came to the place of realising that the stroke was heaven-sent because she was mentally and emotionally spring-cleaning all the ick from the past. We soon reached a point where she had a previously-unseen vision of what we called *Future-Doreen*. This Doreen was a happy, fit, healthy, inspired and inspiring woman and mother, working as a positive change worker and feeling fabulous about life.

When I asked her unconscious mind if it would be OK to create this, even though that was what she consciously wanted, she felt her body have a, "No," response and heard the word *No* inside her head.

So I asked: Avoiding *Future-Doreen* for what purpose?

Doreen: She'll be alone, disapproved of.

Me: Avoiding disapproval for what purpose?

Doreen: To feel loved and accepted.

Me: And arriving in that place of feeling totally loved and accepted, what would be possible?

Doreen: I could be myself.

Me: And with that permission to be yourself, would it be ok for us to explore what's holding you back from allowing yourself to be happy, fit, healthy, inspired and inspiring, and feeling fabulous about life?

Doreen: Yes . . .

We revisited a time in childhood where she'd been a dog in her school play. I watched as she remembered the actual performance and her smile glowed. She'd remembered doing some ad-libbing when her tail got caught in a prop-door and "little-Doreen" just loved the whole experience, singing and dancing, being part of the team and the enthusiastic applause at the end. Each of the characters bowed individually at the conclusion of the performance and the applause for the dog was most definitely the loudest! Full of confidence and pride she got off the stage to her mother and was met with a disgusted parent who told her that she was totally embarrassed to be the mother of *that* girl in the dog costume who was so full of herself. When Doreen got to this part of the story, I watched her body language shift into the body language I'd first seen when she walked into my clinic. Even though she was recalling this event as an adult and understanding it with the benefit of hindsight, her body still responded like the 10 year old girl; crushed and deciding that it's not ok to be in the moment and love shining from the inside out.

So, in her adult life prior to working with me, when she'd been wanting to be on stage or do anything out of her comfort zone a little voice inside her head would say it was wrong, or not to look like she was loving herself. She would get angry with that voice and tell it to piss off (just like I was taught to when the Ego raises its ugly head) or believe it and just do nothing. From my perspective, our unconscious programming was put together over time and, yes, quite often it can be child-like. When in the presence of a child wanting to be accepted and loved for who they are, do you think telling them to "piss off" is the best possible choice? What this voice inside Doreen needed to hear was that it's OK. "Little Doreen" needed to understand that her mother loved her and was just parenting her from her own beliefs about being seen to be full of yourself. In her mother's 'programming' it was a bad thing. I had Doreen do a visualisation exercise to communicate with her own unconscious mind. She closed her eyes and imagined that she could travel all the way back into that event right into the moment after the dog had received its huge applause and have a talk with "little-Doreen" . . . and say everything that her younger self needed to hear.

She visualised floating in and landing back stage, in time to introduce herself to "little-Doreen" (before she saw her Mum). She used this moment to share all that was in her heart: *"I've come all the way back from the future to this moment to tell you, that you, sweetheart, are amazing and talented, and I saw what you did when your tail got caught and how you made it part of the show so not only were you talented and a pleasure to watch, but you were also able to think on your feet because you're intelligent and you were totally in the flow of the performance and of life and I am so proud of you."* And she hugged her with all the love in her heart for this adventurous, gifted, clever little girl who was so proud of herself in that moment. Then she sat her down and told her some truths about her Mum. *"Sweetheart, when your Mum was a small girl, most parents wanted their children to be quiet and never draw attention to themselves, so the little girl inside your Mum, just like you're inside of me, tells her that it's not ok to be loud or proud, that those things are really bad, and because she loves you, that little girl inside your Mum is going to say something like that to you in a minute. When she does, know it's just the little girl, younger than you are now, telling you to draw less attention to yourself, because that was the way that she got to experience love. When you hear what your Mum is going to say, please remember all that we've spoken about and understand that this is your Mum's way of trying to make sure you fit in with her parents' vision of what a lovable child is and not actually anything about reality going on now. Remember the loud, enthusiastic applause from the other people, adults, in the room who are proud of you, remember how amazing you feel right now and know that it's like a shield. In years to come, your Mum will be as proud of you as you are right now, but she just hasn't gone through that process of re-parenting her little girl yet."*

It wasn't long after this session that *Future-Doreen*, in the present day, did another public performance. I had the pleasure of being there and I sat with my children next to her mother who was looking at her daughter in a whole new way—with respect and pride.

We can all experience moments of fear—fear of failure or fear of success. We can all disconnect from our amazingness and question our worth. What if that was just OK to do? What if you stopped judging yourself and just took those moments as the feedback system that they are?

Asking yourself: "For what purpose?" or "What is the positive benefit I get from feeling this way?" is a wonderful way to open yourself up to the resources of your unconscious wisdom.

Your unconscious mind is incredibly powerful. I have worked with countless couples referred to me from a fertility clinic to release unconscious blocks with conceiving. In so many of these sessions we uncovered a positive benefit to remaining in the current situation. When you can be supported to meet this need (whatever the positive benefit was) in a new way then the unconscious mind can relax and allow pregnancy to occur. In the same way I've worked with countless clients experiencing serious illness who have, through their work with me, been able to uncover a positive benefit to remaining ill. When this need is met in new ways, the body heals itself and life goes on. Please know that I am talking here about clients who have had unconscious blocks or limitations and this does not apply to all cases of infertility or illness.

Use the tools in this book to feel as good as you possibly can right now and then the action you want to take will be easier and create better results. If you consistently run into a block then get support to release it but, please, speak nicely to yourself inside your head. It's wonderful to be a work-in-progress. The more you acknowledge your sticking points and take action to get unstuck (like you are by reading this book), the more empowered and resourceful you become and the lighter and happier you can feel about yourself and about your life.

Today's Commitment to Authentic Personal Power

If you happen to be in a *non-blurkey* place right now then today is just for reading.

The instructions that follow are for next time you're in that *blurk* place, if it's right now, then get to it right away. If not, then keep for future reference but always remember that there is always a positive intention for your *blurkiness* and you get to choose what to do about it.

1) Acknowledge your state of mind and state of being—what's it like, mentally, physically and energetically?

2) Answer these questions: Feeling this way for what purpose?

3) What are the positive benefits I get from feeling/staying this way?

4) Do I wholeheartedly wish to be experiencing these benefits? And if so, can I meet these needs in a new way?

5) If I continue to be in this state, what will I successfully avoid?

6) Do I wholeheartedly wish to avoid this experience? And if so, could I choose to have a different avoidance strategy without having to create this *blurky* feeling?

7) If I continue to be in this state whose attention will I receive?

8) Do I wholeheartedly wish to receive their attention in this way? And if not, what are three other ways that I could attract and receive their attention without having to create this *blurky* feeling?

9) If I continue to be in this state, whose attention will I avoid? (If you get an answer then cycle back up to questions 2 and 3, but with the question of "avoiding for what purpose?")

10) How old do I feel in this space?

11) What can I think, say, feel or do that will begin to create the shift I *know* I can create?

At the end of this book is a list of ways to "Uplift Your Moment." As you know, when you create a shift towards feeling empowered this uplifts your thinking, your mood and your resulting actions. In the future, once you've read this book cover to cover, you will be able to come back to today if you're having a *blurky* moment, answer the questions for yourself and connect to the awareness that your unconscious mind is creating for you. Sometimes *blurkiness* can be a signal that you're overdoing it and need some down time. Sometimes it's a signal that you've had too much downtime and you need to get moving. Sometimes it has nothing to do with up or down time and is about fears or insecurities or a whole host of other reasons. Answering the questions will create the awareness. You can also flick to the back and choose one of the "Uplift Your Moment"—activities to create the shift in your state.

Day 17

You Create Your Reality

You are in charge of your paint brush and pallet

You are the writer, the director and play the lead role in your reality. I love this as a metaphor because it's one we can all understand.

We create our reality using the three ingredients discussed in this book. As you already know, you are creating your experiences with your mind. You will be learning how your body and vibration are also vital parts of the life-creation process in the coming days.

I have been through a long and arduous journey with the concept that I create my reality. It has been a driving force of the inspiration for creating this book!

First – I learned it.

Then – I blamed myself for choosing all the painful events of my past and current reality.

And next – I embraced that without those hurts I wouldn't have become 'the me' that I now love being and found my way into the best work on the planet (helping people to love themselves and create lives they love!)

And then . . . I used this concept to trap myself in very dissatisfying personal situations by deciding that I was creating, for some higher purpose, all of the dysfunction.

I used to see the concept of creating my own reality very literally, rather than understanding that in every relationship there is an opportunity to learn and practice self-worth and set boundaries for how I would agree to be treated. I had the life-changing epiphany while living in a share house with a girlfriend. She had two pets (a cat and a huge puppy) and was rarely home. She would often drop in for two minutes, feed the animals and leave again, or just phone and ask me to feed them without walking the energetic puppy or spending any time with her cat.

One weekend, her cat took to my vintage, red velvet arm-chair and ripped open one of the sides. And the puppy ate two sides of my mattress base and did number two on my carpeted floor. When I got home and saw what happened, I was really angry. When she got home and I told her what happened, rather than apologising or offering to replace anything she laughed and said: "Wow, what's going on with you that you're choosing to create all of that!?" And that was all there was to it, from her perspective. This was something that I alone had manifested and she didn't see that she had any part in it whatsoever.

There are some people who embrace the 'new age' movement as an opportunity to take responsibility for absolutely nothing whilst proclaiming that they are helping others to take full responsibility for their actions. Have you come across this in your life? In my part of the world, it is often expressed by people saying, "That's their shit; it's got nothing to do with me!" While everyone has 'stuff' – a pre-existing program and ways of interpreting events – it doesn't mean that you should totally discount the effect you have on the people around you (assuming that you want to keep those people around you). It also doesn't mean you have to take 100% responsibility for everything everyone experiences. You are in charge of *just you*. In the situation described above, I chose to continue living with someone who had pets that weren't looked after to the standard I was comfortable with. I was at home more than my housemate, but I hadn't decided to get any animals myself because I didn't have the time to dedicate to them and so I resented being caught in my own dilemma of wanting the animals to be loved and not being willing to prioritise the spare time I had into someone else's. I was fearful of the damage the dog was doing to the yard, because it was a rental property, but was so dedicated to avoiding conflict that I never spoke to my housemate about it. So yes, there were lots of things going on for me that created this experience and there were lots of opportunities for me to learn how to do it differently.

Creating your reality does not mean you should sit in the effect of your causes and feel stupid. Creating your reality means that what happens around you reflects your existing beliefs about yourself and about life. How you choose to respond to all the events you *co*-create is your choice.

So now, in my current view of 'you create your own reality,' I understand that everything I experience around me is all that I've agreed to have around me, attracted in and chose to keep. If there's something I'm not enjoying, I have choices. I've arrived in the heartfelt place of understanding that I *am* the writer, director and lead role in the movie of my life. I appreciate that I, like all beings here on planet Earth, am a work in progress and that it is only through the process of trial and correction that we learn and I create learning experiences for myself every time I take action. This action is part of being alive and without it, I would be creating stagnation. So, I choose life and learning and understand that process without judgment.

If I were ever living again with someone else's untrained, bored and lonely pets that were destroying my stuff, I would now have a range of tools I could choose to use. I could express that when my things were damaged by their pets, I expect them to be replaced. I could share that I find it difficult to live with animals that are being treated differently to the way that my values dictate that animals should be treated. I could set a boundary that they had to stay outside when my housemate wasn't at home. I could make sure my door was always closed and not contribute my favourite furniture to communal areas. And if the boundaries just weren't workable, well I could choose to make new living arrangements. Back then I didn't even know what I wanted because I was going about agreeing with what other people wanted. Now I have the skills to communicate my needs, my fears and hurts when they arise.

So, are you using this concept that you create your reality to feel inspired with all the power you have to change things? Or are you using it as a way to feel awful about what you've created? It's time, isn't it, for more of the former, and less of the latter?

I know it's strange, that in the field of personal development, so many people use this concept to avoid any actual personal development, "That's their shit; it's got nothing to do with me!" In life, we learn the most about ourselves in relationships with other people. The greatest personal development comes when our relationships teach us what's working and what's not. If everyone always agreed with you, it might feel nice in the moment, but what would you be learning? If you have conflict in your life, what can you learn from it, other than blaming the other person?

Looking around at your life, right now, what is it like?

Remember back to Day 4—How You've Created Your *Now*.

What would you like your *now* to look like in six months' time?

What would you like your *now* to look like in twelve months' time?

How about in five years' time?

You are in charge of the quality of the *now* you're experiencing and creating for future *nows*. You might not get to choose what the other players are doing in their games of life, because everyone has free will and gets to choose for themselves (what and how they want to play) but you do get to choose the game for you. And life is a team sport. Even people who choose to live without any close personal relationships are still reading books written by other people, having their mail delivered by other people and probably eating food grown by other people. So while you can't choose how you want your existing team to be, you can choose who are the most influential players and exercise behavioural flexibility when interacting with them.

Remember this:

Your state of being mentally, physically and energetically, your behaviour and your ways of communicating are always part of the pattern that drives your experiences. There is power in that, a gentle powerful permission to be you. If you're not being authentically yourself, then you are creating relationships and life circumstances that will not be satisfying and joyous and you're missing out on being known and loved for all that you are.

Today's Commitment to Authentic Personal Power

For the next 24 hours observe yourself and your interactions. Aim to see yourself on an objective level. In what circumstances do you feel at *cause*? Who are you with and what are you thinking, feeling and doing? In what circumstances do you feel at *effect*? Who are you with and what are you thinking, feeling and doing? If you end up saying mean things to yourself inside your head – what brings that on and what do you choose to do about it?

The purpose of today is to be aware – when are you experiencing the truth that you create your reality? Are you using that truth to feel like a *twit* (for creating whatever silly thing is happening) or to feel empowered by the learning experience?

Before moving on to Day 18 take some notes about your observations.

What did you notice?

Upon reflection, what were the three most valuable insights from these hours of observation and awareness?

1)

2)

3)

DAY 18

The Life Force Within and All around You

Nothing is solid—everything is
alive with moving energy

Physicists acknowledge that the entire Universe is made up of energy vibrating at different frequencies. As we are beings in this energetic universe, we too are infused with, powered and supported by this energy. We as people have many varied understandings of and beliefs about this energy of life and my intention for today is not to meddle with any existing spiritual or religious beliefs you have. Likewise, if you don't have any solid spiritual or religious beliefs, I won't be suggesting you take on any. The purpose of today is to bring this energy of life into conscious awareness. Through today and continuing on days 19 and 20, we are going to consider, observe and experience this energy in your body and life experiences. We are going explore how this energy can empower you to direct the 'now' and your future.

The life-force is an intelligent, organising energy that exists within and all around you. Nothing is solid, even this book is just atoms hanging out in just the right combinations close enough together to appear as a solid to the human eye. This energy exists in many layers and densities so to explain it well we will need to briefly mention a few of these levels.

Firstly, let's look at an atom:

carbon atom

- electron
- proton
- neutron

Every cell of your body is made up of atoms—positively or negatively charged particles spinning around repelling or attracting each other. Look now at one of your hands: that physical thing in front of you, just like the rest of your body and every 'solid' object you see, is made up mostly of space . . . the space in between those teensy tiny positively or negatively charged particles moving together in the synchronized dance of life. If all that space were to disappear, and all the electrons stuck like glue to the protons and neutrons in the centre, like with a neutron star, you would end up small indeed (and quite dense—haha!). To put this in perspective "If you were to crush a 50m Olympic size swimming pool into neutron star material, it would be about 0.05mm long, which is about the width of a single hair." *http://www.askamathematician.com/2011/01/q-if-atoms-are-made-up-of-electrons-protons-and-neutrons-and-the-majority-of-the-volume-of-an-atom-is-space-why-do-things-appear-solid/*

I'm not sure about you, but I'm smaller than a swimming pool, so think about this: If you were only physical matter, without life-force energy, you would be a whole lot smaller than a single hair.

Let that idea wash through you for a moment.

It is the positively and negatively charged vibration of particles and the life-force in between that creates all the things you see, feel and experience.

Energy is a real, dynamic part of your existence; it is in fact, *most* of your existence. Using the example of the swimming pool, the part of you that is actual physical matter (the protons, neutrons and electrons) would probably be invisible to the human eye if it weren't for the energy and vibration of life supporting the existence of your physical body. By choosing to think in terms of only physical, three dimensional *stuff* you are missing out on the true essence of who and what you are—an energetic being that is currently in human form.

Our solar system is not dissimilar to the structure of an atom, and it in turn is part of a galaxy . . . and all just a part of our Universe. We, the planets, stars and even the galaxy are made of the same ingredients and the life-force energy runs through us all.

Our Solar System

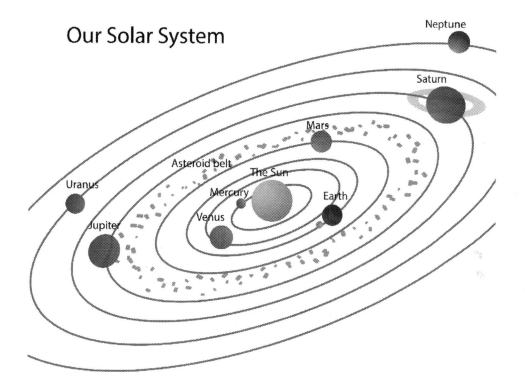

If you're ever feeling stuck and solid and immovable again, remember about the Olympic sized swimming pool . . . and imagine all the energy moving, right now, throughout your being. Where there's energy flowing and moving, positive changes can take place. If your physical body isn't solid then your self-definition shouldn't be either.

> Imagine all that space inside you . . .
>
> How does knowing about it open your perception
> and expectations of what's possible for you?
>
> Can it make your issues seem less solid, too?

So, this energy is within and all around you, but you also have your own individual cell of life-force energy. To introduce this point, I'll start by asking you this: "What's the difference between you and a dead person?"

A spiritual teacher asked me this question back in the late 1990's. I was many years into my personal development journey and at that time, I really thought I understood about the life-force. I had even gone through a long process of releasing my judgments about atrocities performed in the name of organised religions and become comfortable with the word 'God', but being asked this question opened a new understanding for me.

So, what is the difference between you and a dead person?

After the physical stuff is done, there's no heartbeat, brain waves etc I was left with the realisation that it was the life-force that had left the body. I'd used the term life-force for *years* without really ever thinking about what it meant. Like electricity to a light globe, the life-force inside you right this minute is what animates your physical being—the light globe is switched to 'on'. When someone passes away, their life-force energy dissipates and is no longer in their physical body. They simply are not there in their physical body anymore, the body is an empty shell, rather like a light globe that's finished its life and the electricity can no longer power it up. I had the honour of seeing my grandmother's empty physical shell just after she passed over and it was so clear to me that *she* was no longer there. I really understood that day that she was never just her physical body and the part that truly was *her* was no longer there. To make the distinction really clear, there was still universal energy generating all the space in that no-longer-necessary physical shell because it was still made up of atoms (and she didn't disappear, Yoda-style, as she passed over). The part that had left was her individual condensed cell of life-force energy, what many would refer to as her soul.

So, on the atomic level, nothing is solid, and therefore, there are no actual boundaries between people and things and the planet and the universe as a whole. This is why, in spiritual studies we hear the terms "there is no separation" and "we are all one." However, we, as human beings, do have our own life-force energy. We *are* separate beings—otherwise we'd all be clones, thinking the same thing—and you only have to go to a group meeting of any kind to see that we are all fabulously unique.

Your amazing mind can use this idea of being a part of the whole Universe to feel small and insignificant or to feel incredibly honoured to have this chance to be here, now on planet Earth to learn and grow as a being. For me, all that space inside my being means I quite literally cannot be stuck in anything. Whether it be a thought, a feeling, a relationship, a job or a physical size and shape, nothing in the Universe is static and unchangeable so it is an illusion to believe, even for a moment, that I can be stuck and unchangeable in *anything*. Can you feel the freedom that comes from knowing that?

There are no edges or boundaries to this energy, no static ending or beginning. In this way we *are* all part of the whole, whether you want that to be part of a spiritual belief system or not.

So to recap, the whole universe is energy vibrating at different frequencies. This energy organizes particles and maintains structures. Life-force energy also condenses into life forms as individual units.

Now we move to the third way we're going to be talking about life-force energy. Life-force energy flows through the human body, as if it were following an invisible circulatory system. As a teacher of qi gong (an ancient Chinese health care system that unites breathing with physical movements) for over a decade I have taught many students about this flow of life-force energy through the physical body. How fast and free this energy flows in your body relates directly to how light and free you feel. The slower the energy and the more stagnation in this energetic system, the slower everything works and the heavier you feel. The transformations I have witnessed in my classroom teaching qi gong have been amazing. The combination of breathing, movement and focused intention lifts energy and fuels healing on all levels. I've seen disease states change for the better, pain disappear and mental attitudes completely transform through this practice.

I also teach Reiki (a modality that uses life-force energy for restoring and maintaining health) and have worked with clients using other energy healing methods with remarkable transformations. One of my favourite parts of this work is watching what happens when a person realises, perhaps as you are today, that they are not the physical being they thought they were. Knowing about and learning to recognise, use and direct this energy is life-changing for your ongoing personal development.

There are many healing techniques and modalities that support the body's health and vitality by freeing up this energy flow. It excites me greatly that modalities like Chinese medicine and acupuncture, tai chi and shiatsu are being recognised for the results they achieve.

Florence Nightingale first said: "Where there's life there's hope," and I agree wholeheartedly. Where there is energy movement there is potential for dynamic vitality. The universe is in a constant state of movement and transformation and so are you.

Today's Commitment to Authentic Personal Power

You will need to keep track of time with this exercise; so set an alarm of some kind to go off after five minutes and start the timer once you've read all the instructions. You can do this exercise every day or just once, you can do it for one minute or an hour or however long you like, but for today, at least once, please set aside five minutes and go for it. You do not need to be alone, heck you could do it sitting on a crowded train, but you do need for no one to interrupt you with anything that you need to respond to.

If you read through the instructions and think you'll be opening your eyes every few seconds to be checking back in with them then I'd suggest you do this exercise with another person, who reads you the instructions, leaving a minute for you to follow each step before reading the next or record yourself reading them and use that.

During this exercise breathe as slowly as you comfortably can, in and out through your nose. Be willing to accept the running commentary of your mind if it is present. Allow yourself to be inquisitive and open to newness.

Gently close your eyes . . . focus your attention on the skin of your feet and slowly expand that focus up your legs and throughout the skin over your body . . . ask yourself: does my skin feel the same all over? Or different in some places? Can I feel the life-force energy movement there?

Take your mental focus further inward and feel all that space underneath your skin and throughout your body . . . the part you may have previously thought of as the 'physical' you . . . Feel the energy that is actually you . . . and ask yourself: does it feel the same all the way through? Or different in some places? Can I feel the life-force energy movement in there?

Follow the inflow of your breath . . . how does it feel in my energy as I breathe in? . . . What can I sense as my breath flows in . . . and out?

Lastly, take your focus back to your skin . . . how does it feel just outside your skin? . . . Is there anything within five centimetres of your skin, but not touching you? Can you sense that, without feeling it physically?

Imagine your body at the atomic level and your surroundings at the atomic level, too . . . and ask yourself: where do I end? . . . and where does the 'outside' begin? . . . How am I being affected by the energy around me? . . . and how am I affecting the energy around me? . . .

Just breathe . . . and offer your attention to these experiences . . . and your new awareness's . . .

Before moving on, take note of what you noticed and experienced with this exercise. How will those new perceptions lead to different thinking, feeling and actions?

If you liked it, put a note in your diary to remind yourself to do it again.

DAY 19

The Frequency of
Thoughts and Emotions

*Your own energy level is something
that is actually quite tangible and recognisable.*

Everything in the Universe is vibrating energy and your thoughts and emotions are part of that also. Even in standard, everyday conversations (not just the ones taking place at spiritual gatherings) people comment on feeling burdened by circumstances or needing to lighten the load a little by delegating some tasks. This is because some thoughts and feelings have a low vibration and make you feel heavy. At other times, the exact same person, still having all the same responsibilities can 'bounce' into their workplace feeling light and energised. This can happen from one day to the next or depending on what happens during the day, from one moment to the next. A single phone call or thought can create heaviness or lightness—have you noticed this in yourself? Think now of the difference between a bad-news phone call and a fantastic-news phone call.

During a period of time when a close family member was in palliative care, I received a phone call at 2am. On my way from the bed to the phone I felt a constricted, heavy dread as I was expecting to hear very sad news because of the time of the call. I picked the phone up to my sister, who was out having the night of her life, who'd rung to tell me she'd just gotten engaged to her now husband. As you can imagine, I no longer needed that constricted, heavy dread, so the frequency of my thoughts and emotions changed instantly. Had I stopped on the way to the phone that morning and weighed myself before answering the call and afterwards, my physical weight would not have shifted in those few minutes, but energetically I felt like I lost the elephant sitting on my heart as soon as I heard my sister's happy voice.

Yesterday we talked about different forms of life-force energy and today we're going to talk about your energy field. Depending on what you are thinking and feeling your energy field will feel heavy or light. It can also feel constricted or open and free.

169

If you drive a car, you will have had many experiences of driving up to an orange light. There are times where the choice is obvious, you are going to slow down and stop or keep right on driving. And there is a middle ground—the will-I-or-won't-I-spot. If you are a law-abiding citizen and are repelled by the idea of running a red light (be it the financial penalty or just doing something naughty) you will have an energetic experience when you are in that will-I-won't-I space because there are consequences for either choice. If there's someone less careful behind you, they might be expecting you to go through and if you do go through you may not make it. Imagine now, being in that orange-light position and mentally drive through the intersection, not knowing if you're going to be breaking the law or not . . .

Do you experience a feeling of constriction? If you day dream that you make it through while orange, do you experience relief of that constriction and feel more light and open energetically? If you day dream that it goes red right before you drive in and you know that you've been caught . . . what happens to your energy?

Most of the clients I have seen who have been diagnosed with depression are actually experiencing an energetic heaviness and darkness. Their thoughts and feelings are of such a low vibration that just existing feels hard and almost too much to bear. In most cases by working on their unconscious programmed thinking, shifts and changes happen for the better. As these clients step into *cause* it releases hopelessness and creates hope. All thoughts and feelings have a vibration—feel the energetic difference in you, just saying those two words: hopelessness . . . hope . . . they feel different just to say and most definitely to feel. Just like in this book, my work with clients is always wholistic—working with the mind, the energy and the body. Depression is an energetic experience that we can all have from time to time and that takes hold in other cases, in a way that feels more permanent. In most cases I have seen, this depression is brought about by the past or current circumstances of the mind, body and energy. It can be transformed in the same way by empowering all three levels of life experience.

"Where there's hope there's life," Anne Frank.

So, to summarise, all thoughts and feelings have a vibration that affect your energy field and you will have already experienced throughout your life the sensations of heavy, light, constricted and open and free.

You may have noticed these sensations in other people also. Do you have people in your life who are usually uplifting to be around, even if they're not saying much, and others who often feel draining or heavy to be around, even if they're not saying much? You are experiencing their energy field connecting with your own.

We are now going to move on to the next concept, which is: the vibration of all thoughts and feelings are magnetic. This means that all thoughts attract more thoughts of the same type/vibration and all feelings attract more feelings of the same type/vibration. Put simply, if you are having an icky, *blurky* thought you will very easily attract in another thought that matches the vibration you're in and continue to feel the same way; however, you now understand your mind and mental programming more than before. And you have a better understanding of your life-force energy and the role it plays. Does it make sense to you that an angry thought about something in your 'now' easily attracts pre-existing angry thoughts that you have stored in your unconscious mind? And your mind is powerful enough to project out into the future and imagine scenarios, that have not yet occurred, in which you will have the opportunity to continue feeling angry—maybe even MORE angry than how you feel now. Does it make sense to you that when you're feeling happy and excited about something in your 'now' that those thoughts and resulting feelings easily attract pre-existing happy and excited thoughts you have stored in your unconscious mind? And your mind is powerful enough to project out into the future and imagine scenarios, that have not yet occurred, in which you will have the opportunity to continue to feel happy and excited—maybe even MORE happy and excited than how you feel now.

Like attracts like. This is why knowing that you are an energetic being is so important. When you can uplift your vibration, you will be easily able to access the uplifted thoughts and feelings that you already have available. Whatever vibration you are in, you're inviting more and more of exactly the same stuff into your 'now'.

"The definition of insanity is doing the same thing over and over and expecting a different result," Albert Einstein.

Thoughts and emotions are magnetic. Whatever you're experiencing will attract in more of the same, just like if you throw a bit of bread at a single seagull you will attract 100 of them in moments.

Your entire being is a sending and receiving station—transmitting thoughts and radiating vibrations and receiving in the same. In Day 18, you read about everything being made up of energy and today I want to tell you that the energy is measureable and there is a whole lot of very interesting science exploring the tangible reality that thoughts are 'things' and that the frequency of our food, emotions and surrounding environment have major impacts on our physical, mental and energetic bodies.

Not only are you a sending and receiving station, but you are also in possession of a whole-being tuning system that you can use to tune into the frequency of your choice. You have so much power, in each and every moment to choose what you are tapping into.

Just like your ears respond to vibration and we call it hearing, your entire being responds to the vibration within and all around you and I call this living.

The idea that energy is intelligent and can carry information is evident in mobile phone conversations and the World Wide Web—intangible connections that we trust to have our conversations and move our money around. We expect to pick up the television or radio show of our choice when we turn it on to the right frequency (channel). If colours, shapes, sounds and digits of information can be sent on invisible waves around the globe, sometimes bouncing off satellites in orbit around the planet, can it make sense that people can sense each other's feelings, even when they are far apart geographically? Can it make sense that you can think of a person right before they ring you?

The Universe is made up of life force energy, the vital building blocks of life. Your individual essence is also pure in the same way. As human beings we have this amazing mind that can tune into this vitality or disconnect from it. We can use our mind as the powerful life-invigorating tool that it is and understand that we are part of life itself. Or we can see things in a very physical way and miss out on the vitality of experiencing our true essence.

Calming thoughts allows your essence (the truth of who you are without mental constructs that say you are separate, alone or in any way less beautiful than the rest of nature) to be recharged by the life-force energy it is made up of. Like dirty water can be flushed clean in the presence of rushing flows of pure, clean, fresh water.

Your mind is not dirty; it is just very powerful, as it allows you to connect with your strength, power, hope, inspiration or your perceived weaknesses, disempowerment, hopelessness and depression.

Today's Commitment to Authentic Personal Power

1) Take a moment to remember the times in your life when you've felt down and heavy, or uplifted and light. There has been no difference in the actual weight or shape of your physical body in these moments, but it feels so physical when one is weighed down by the world.

What experiences in your life have generated the heaviest feelings?

What experiences in your life have generated the most lightness?

Does just remembering these experiences recreate some of that heaviness or lightness in your body right now?

2) Throughout the next 24 hours, notice how your thoughts are making you feel, but rather than naming the emotion e.g. "Man, I'm feeling really cranky right now" or "Wow, I'm feeling really happy, for no reason that I can think of," I want for you to notice how you feel energetically. Do you feel heavy or light? Do you feel contracted or expanded? Do you feel trapped or stagnant or free as a bird (one that's actually free, not one of those caged ones)—you get the idea!

It is incredibly valuable to notice how you are feeling energetically, because it's yet another guidance system, letting you know that your current circumstances are really working for you or to let you know: "Oi! It's time to change something! You can feel a lot better than this!" And by the end of this book, you'll have a lot of tools for lifting your vibration and getting into the light, expanded, free place where it's so easy to feel fantastic.

DAY 20

Your Personal Frequency

How it alters your perceptions, thoughts,
feelings & resulting actions

Think of your individual essence of life-force energy as a pod that is vibrating on a specific frequency at all times. Like watching a freshly poured glass of fizzy lemonade, this life-force energy is in constant motion and responds instantly to your conscious and unconscious mind and also what you are doing with your physical body. All thoughts, feelings and actions have an individual and specific vibration. Feeling angry has a vibration, and as we know, certain sensations in your body radiate from you matching that vibration. Feeling joyful bliss has a very different, faster and uplifted vibration, generating very different sensations in the body that radiate from you.

We have already talked about how your body (when resonating in the vibration of anger) is able to easily access all of your own unresolved anger from the past and imagine future events to get angry about. It is also true that when angry, it's very easy to tap into and absorb other people's anger, and interpret current situations in a way as to cause you to feel even angrier. Likewise, when you are in the vibration of love and compassion, the same is true—it is natural and easy to tap into and absorb other people's love and compassion and interpret current situations in a way that allows more love and compassion into your being. Today we take that to a new place and see how the exact same situation can be interpreted by you angrily or with compassion depending on the vibration you are in when it happens.

The difference between looking out at your life and seeing your positive and wonderful circumstances and looking out at your life and thinking it totally sucks is often the vibration you're in.

Many years ago I did a lot of work with a single mother of three, very young children. Depending on where her vibration was at she could feel intelligent, sexy, accomplished and proud of her life—a homeowner, working in her dream job, healthy and positive OR she could feel like a slow-learning, old, shabby, mutton-dressed-as-lamb, financially hopeless, lonely single woman. The exact same circumstances can lead to wildly different perceptions. She felt the I'm-on-top-of-things feelings when she was getting enough sleep, eating healthy food, exercising, and maintaining her daily practice of qi gong. She would feel completely the opposite if she wasn't doing all of these healthy activities. In the higher vibrational frequencies she had very positive views of herself and her future; she'd set goals, create plans, take actions and be confident of achieving the next level of her success. In lower vibrations she'd feel like quitting her dream job because perhaps she wasn't really that good at it and hadn't really done anything new in it or achieved the goals she'd set, so why bother. She'd judge herself as all talk and no action and just want to eat another litre of ice-cream or block of chocolate because she felt horrible about herself and her life.

Energy breeds energy. Like attracts like. Being in a higher vibration creates a higher quality of perception, thinking and actions. Being in a lower vibration creates a lower quality of perception, thinking, and actions. It's really that simple.

In a higher vibration, she'd want to act on her inspiration and she did. She had actually achieved many successes over the years in her dream job, some of which had created positive national and international attention in her field. In her lower vibration; feeling heavy (and usually tired) she would completely disregard these successes and still feel like an unaccomplished loser. I was so happy that she chose to invest in herself by getting support from me over those years when things were really tough. Often my job was putting her on a healing table, balancing and releasing energetic stagnation and reminding her that there is no substitute for a good night's sleep. She would go weeks at a time without more than a few hours of sleep in a row and have to work the next day and the day after that and so on and yet was expecting that she could maintain the patient parenting she respected and the motivation and inspiration she expected from herself professionally. There are many reasons why we need other people in our lives—Day 31 is all about this, In the case of this client, she needed me to support her (like someone who has taken a dangerous hallucinogenic drug) by constantly reminding her that the things that were seeming real, like her being an unaccomplished loser, were just a delusion brought on by low vibration—it's not real, breathe . . . relax . . . get some sleep and it will soon be over and you'll be back to your amazing self . . . it's all going to be alright.

While this is perhaps a more extreme example than what we experience in normal daily life, we have all, to some extent I'm sure, experienced similar shifts in perception. We all have days or moments when we feel that we're 'on' and can do no wrong and other days or moments when everything is clunky and hard, and awkward and slow.

Having free flowing, high vibration creates responses such as:

- Patience and a long fuse before getting frustrated
- In control and balanced
- Able to easily explain things
- Compassion and understanding
- Feeling connected and resourced
- Empowerment
- Gratitude and appreciation
- Remembering to do positive things for yourself (like taking supplements or doing feel-good tasks you've committed to)
- Wanting to exercise and be in nature
- Being attracted to high quality, healthy food

Having slow moving, low vibration creates responses such as:

- Instant frustration
- Overwhelm
- Completely loosing your cool while trying to explain things (surely people should just KNOW this stuff!!)
- Conflict and judgement
- Feeling disconnected, alone, and not resourceful
- Disempowered
- Unappreciative and unappreciated
- Forgetting to do positive things for yourself (like taking supplements or doing feel-good tasks you've committed to)
- Wanting to be inactive and indoors
- Being attracted to low quality, unhealthy food

In all vibrations we will feel attracted to or most comfortable in and with places and people that match that vibration. This is all well and good, but it does not help when it comes to how you perceive things in a low vibration. For example, if you happen to be feeling angry and frustrated with your wife and you go to the pub, get really drunk and whine about it with some other men down there you are likely to get a vibration back that matches the one you are in.

However, if you happened to feel angry and frustrated with your wife so you go for a run on the beach or through the forest with huge, old trees you might start to feel differently. Then if you went and spoke about it with a happy friend who is in a marriage that you admire for its strength, shared love and values you might come home with a whole new perception and perhaps be at *cause* for communicating your feelings or changing something in yourself to create changes in your relationship (or both!).

I have some clients who come and see me with paperwork in hand. It is a list of all the issues going on and all the stuff they need to talk with me about during the session. Often, about half an hour in, as they have shifted totally from their original vibration into something much more enjoyable, they pull the list out and can laugh about most of the points, no longer needing any external assistance with them. It's not that we've already discussed the issues written down, it's just that the client is feeling so much better, connected to their resources, positive and empowered and now realises that they can very easily handle it all perfectly well and our session transforms into something else.

Today's Commitment to Authentic Personal Power

Your vibration is a major influence in your perception as you go about the world as a meaning-maker. On Day 18, you experienced feeling your energy right now and understanding yourself as a mostly energetic being. Next you reflected on how your vibration has created heaviness and lightness throughout your past and got to practice noticing it in your 'now', as you went throughout your day.

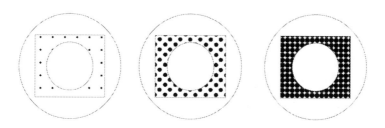

Today I want you to look at these diagrams and see if you can use them to create more lightness in your body. So whatever state you're in right now I want you to follow these instructions:

1) Close your eyes and imagine that within your body is a circle filled with pure, high vibrational life—force energy.

2) Then, imagine a square around your whole body that's filled with dots of whatever density seems right to you. The dots represent your thoughts and the density/heaviness of your vibration.

Outside that square is another circle that represents the pure, high vibrational life-force energy that exists all around you and throughout the universe. The energy in this outer circle is a perfect vibrational match for the energy within the circle that's inside your body. It is the density of those dots (the density of your vibration) that connects or disconnects you from the high vibration in the outer circle.

3) Breathe in and out as slowly and deeply as is comfortable and imagine the dots, one by one, winking out and disappearing. See the box around your body getting clearer and clearer, more and more open and free from dots. This is allowing the vibration of the box that surrounds your body to slowly begin matching the vibration of the circle inside you and the larger circle outside the square.

4) As more space opens up, imagine that circle inside you, which represents you and your pod of concentrated life-force energy, opening up and expanding out into the space now available in the square.

Imagine that it gets bigger with every breath in—and that can make sense because as you breathe in, your body expands.

Imagine that it also gets bigger with every breath out—and that can make sense because your out breath is energy moving outwards, creating movement just like when you blow out a candle, and in this exercise your breath is pushing the boundary of your circle out further.

Expand your pod out as far as you can while still feeling comfortable. That might be as far as the edges of the room you're in or all the way around the planet—it's up to you.

How does it feel as you intentionally create expansion?

You can use this as a technique throughout the day if you're feeling constricted and heavy as it can be done in just a minute or two of focused intention. If you get well-practiced at this technique you can easily do it with eyes open and in any circumstances. For now though, shut your eyes and feel the vibrational effects.

Day 21

"Feeling" vs. Physiological Sensations

*What's the difference between anxiety, excitement, and the
sensation of vibrational growth and expansion?*

Your body is a sensational collection of intelligent machinery; it sends out and gathers information constantly using all of its resources. We also know that thinking and feeling are physical experiences (as well as energetic ones) and today this will come together in a new way.

Have you ever felt anxious?

How do you know that you're actually feeling anxious?

If you think of your whole body in terms of sensations and feedback, what happens throughout your body when you're experiencing what you'd label as "anxious"? Rather than words that describe feelings, try using words like this:

Hot	Cold	Light
Heavy	Sharp	Spiky
Buzzy	Squirmy	Gooey
Open	Constricted	Fluttery

Where are these sensations in your body?

Do they move? If so, where do they start and where do they go?

Have you ever experienced one or more of these sensations, but you just didn't know how you felt? Have you ever started crying and been unsure why?

On Day 5, you learned about being a *meaning-making machine*. You are also doing this when you interpret physiological sensations and label them as a feeling. We talented human beings have super-fast processing minds fully equipped for jumping to conclusions . . . and so we do. The conclusions we reach are based on our existing *program* so sometimes (or maybe even lots of times) we are unaware of the newness of experiences and jump to the conclusion that we're having the same old feelings by interpreting our physiological sensations incorrectly.

Feelings are real; I'm not suggesting that you're making them up as you go along. What I am saying is this: when we can take the time to be aware of the way our body is responding to certain circumstances, rather than leaping to conclusions, you can end up with a new awareness of the sensations you are feeling.

As an example, I will share Mark's story with you. Mark came to me with the goal of moving up the corporate ladder. Mark read the books and went to the seminars and understood that by getting his thinking right and keeping his energy clear and high, he could make "magic" happen in his practical life. So, after a few sessions and adopting several lifestyle changes to raise his energy he became more aware and sensitive energetically to what was going on around him. He was feeling a lot better inside himself. Mark started standing taller, walking with more confidence and behaving differently at work. Later, at a work social event, Mark was talking with a group of executives and he shared his views on how the company could easily shift into a new market. They listened, and one of the Directors just stopped, looked up, moved his tongue up against his teeth (so you could see the bulge under his upper lip) and finally said to my client, "You could be onto something there." And that was it. The Director moved off into other conversations and my client, seeing his reaction jumped to some conclusions about everything he was feeling.

Your unconscious mind is a highly efficient information collector. During the conversation, Mark knew the Director was listening, on some deep level unconsciously, he knew that the Director was not only listening but thinking and making pictures inside his mind (with all that looking up) and considering the imagery he was creating. As the Director walked away, my client felt a buzz in his chest and slackness in his arms, his breathing changed, and his mind went blank for a moment. Then, the leap happened; Mark interpreted what he was feeling as anxiety. Once he had labelled the feeling, his *proover department* went to work. His mind (an ever loyal servant) agreed to dig up proof that there was reason to feel anxious so as to prove the interpretation correct. He then reviewed the whole interaction and completely misinterpreted what had gone on, and the anxious feeling grew, he was able to access the shadow of his old not-good-enough stuff and ended up leaving the event.

We debriefed over the weekend, and I took Mark back to the initial reaction and set of physiological sensations. What he was actually feeling was energetic expansion happening in his practical life. The buzz in Mark's chest was the beginning of the excitement that this expansion was creating. The slackness in his arms was the result of all the tension he'd been holding on to instantly leaving his shoulders. Our breath and our mind acknowledge newness as the pattern interrupt that it is. All he needed to do was breathe deeply into that buzz and realise that his whole being was letting him know that his dreams of playing in a bigger pond were being realised. So lying on my healing table, shifting that old interpretation out of his energy, that's what Mark did, and I'll never forget the smile on his face as he acknowledged that buzz as excitement and confirmation that he was onto something new.

I don't want for you to read this and start to mistrust your feelings. What I want is for you to experience the incredible opening of mind, body and energy when we ask questions of ourselves rather than jump to conclusions.

What if the next time you feel a strong emotion, you ask yourself:

What are the physiological sensations I'm experiencing? Remember, not the 'feeling', just the sensations in your being.

What could they mean?

BREATHE DEEPLY . . . Consciously choose to drop your shoulders . . . place your tongue on the bottom of your mouth (it has a pleasant resting place there but will tend to be up on the roof of your mouth if you're doing lots of thinking).

What else could these physiological sensations mean?

What's the most positive interpretation I can make of what's going on?

It might surprise you to know how wildly different emotional states can feel remarkably similar. I mention this, so you know it's OK that you've been misinterpreting sensations sometimes. And here's the thing: whatever you decide you're feeling, your mind will prove you right—that's how your mind works.

Try this right now—wherever you are, whatever time it is, whether you're alone or in a room of people, say these words to yourself three times in a row, "I'm not safe" and see what happens. While I write this (and do the exercise myself) that thought creates the feelings of not being safe—it's not overwhelming fear, but I can notice the shift in physiological sensations. Then I look at the biggest tree I can see from my window and I imagine someone could be behind there, or I become aware of the big open space behind me, and even though I'm home alone, I feel like I want to look over my shoulder. My ears go on super alert for any sounds that I might have missed before I was paying attention to my safety. I feel like I've energetically shrunk just a little bit and my body mirrors that in my posture.

Put the book down and try it for yourself.

What did you experience?

Now, get up and shake that off. Physically if you can, or just imagine a white light coming down in through the top of your head and all the way down through the soles of your feet, cleansing away whatever sensations you experienced—however mild or severe. If white light isn't your thing then jump up and sing a bit of, ♪*shake it up baby now (shake it up baby)*♪*twist and shout* ♫. Or you could choose to stay in that old thought and entertain it and perhaps create yourself a heart-clenching panic, but I suggest you choose the shake it off method instead. As always, it's up to you.

Now try this: say the following words to yourself three times in a row, "I am totally safe and protected." When I say these words my body instantly straightens, my posture improves, and my breathing deepens. I imagine the solidity of the walls of my home and feel the protection they provide from the elements. I feel as though my energy encompasses my whole house and land, and up the street, I feel light and totally safe. Put the book down and try it, and see what happens to you.

The purpose of this exercise is to show you the power of your thoughts and to highlight how misinterpreting your physiological sensations will also lead to having the experience you decided you were having.

I want to mention a few things that will impact on this exercise. Firstly, before embarking on my personal development journey, I had a lot of experience with feeling unsafe. I could turn a perfectly happy park by a lake into a horrifyingly unsafe place with countless hiding places for predators. Developing yourself to be all you can be, does not erase the past. It's still there in the rich tapestry of your unconscious mind, what changes is you don't access the information and create feelings from those places unnecessarily. If you've never felt unsafe, you may have experienced only a very mild change in physiology with the first part of the exercise or no change whatsoever. Likewise, if you have never felt safe and protected, you may not have felt a significant change either.

If you've been unsafe in your past, it might have been a scary and horrible sentence to say and invited some powerful sensations into your experience. If that is so, please choose to see someone, like me, who can help you reroute your unconscious patterns because you are probably feeling like that a lot of the time and you deserve a lot more joy in your life, right now.

Just as one more example, I want to talk about the difference between yearning and sadness. I work with a lot of people who have a yearning for something and for many of them the two words are *synonymous* for the same physiological sensations. I want to take a moment to mention here that yearning is a deep longing, a desire, a thirst for something—this can create fantastic physiology for action if interpreted correctly. If you misinterpret your yearning with sadness you will instead access the parts of your programming that say, "I'll never have that, never get there, never be that," and you'll create a whole being that agrees with you and begin digging up proof that it's true.

In Day 20, I talked about energetic growth and expansion. As you grow and increase your frequency, you also experience physiological sensations too. When you set out a huge goal for yourself and start to take action towards it's achievement, you will experience all kinds of physiological sensations as you call yourself forth to access more positive parts of your unconscious programming and step into the physicality of the 'new' you. It's often by misinterpreting these signals of growth that amazingly talented people stop taking action before allowing themselves to share their gifts with the world around them. That is why today is so important!

I'll never forget the first time I taught a group of forty people. My largest group, prior to that day, was ten. Standing up before them, do you think I experienced some physiological sensations? You betcha! What I was feeling was the energetic expansion that it takes to command the attention of that many beings. I took about three seconds to breathe into that and delivered the content I was passionate about. When I left that class, I felt on top of the world. I'd had an energetic upgrade. I'd accessed the most positive parts of my unconscious programming and I loved the experience. Growth is a wholistic experience—your mind, body and vibration are all having the same experience at the same time. Personal growth will expand your energy and energetic awareness, so it's important to get to know what that feels like.

Today's Commitment to Authentic Personal Power

When you notice changes in your physiological sensations ask yourself the questions below:

What are the physiological sensations I'm experiencing?

What am I making them mean?

Stop a moment and take a deep breath in through your nose and slowly breathe out through your mouth, resting your tongue in the bottom of your mouth (it will generally be touching the roof of your mouth if you're doing lots of thinking).

What else could these physiological sensations mean?

What's the most positive interpretation I can make of what's going on?

Remember, this is just for today. You don't need to do this micromanagement of your physiology for the rest of forever. If you can do it, just for today, then you will have a new unconscious pattern to question yourself when it really matters.

DAY 22

Cause and Effect Part 2

*Other people, angels, guides, spiritual
helpers and your own free will*

You are powerful. I'm sure you've already gotten this message in the previous days and even prior to reading this book. It takes a certain belief in your power to believe that the contents of a book can help you. The book can't reach out into your circumstances and change your life. Any book is only going to work with the innate resources you already have—your body, mind or vibration—and you need to do the rest. So, in an important unconscious way, you already believe in yourself.

So often I see powerful people creating what they believe will happen, all the while wishing that the outside world would deliver something else. I worked with a woman once called Esther who'd felt disempowered all her life. She'd been forced to move schools a lot due to her father's work, and she never wanted to leave the relationships she'd created. In time, she learned not to let anyone in to avoid the hurt she experienced when she felt ripped out of life and planted elsewhere. When we started our work, she'd been married for over 20 years. She was unhappy and dissatisfied in her marriage, she was certain that her husband thought he was better than her in every way and that is why he made all the decisions for them. She had even worked in the job he chose, that she didn't enjoy, for over 10 years. When she found me on the internet she was really sick of her life and described it as empty and meaningless. She said that if she were to die today, nobody would miss *her*; they would just have to look for someone else to perform the tasks she performed for them (even her children were in this category). She and her husband had an active social life that she organised—all the dinners, the restaurants, the barbeques, it all fell down to her and when people were there having a good time, she felt they were just being nice to her and were having a good time because of the other people there. She believed she was merely the humble and excluded organiser of things for others. She deeply wished that her husband would tell her that she could work elsewhere or give her control over some aspect of their life. The fact that he didn't, she interpreted as him thinking she was incapable.

No one outside of you can give you what you, yourself, do not have an opening for. You are in charge of what happens and completely in charge of what you allow in.

People in relationships are in a dance. If you've both been doing the waltz for 30 years and one of you starts doing the tango, yes it will interrupt the dance, but it can continue as the other person embraces the tango too, or you can create a dazzling combination of waltz-tango. We can create anything together when both people want happiness for themselves and the other.

I worked with Esther for months, on every level, tapping in to all of her innate resources. We created new thought patterns and she had homework to put the new thinking into action. One of her first pieces of homework, after her first session, was to stop organising anything socially. It was her birthday in the coming week and as people started calling her and asking, "What are we doing for your birthday," she had to reply with, "I'm not sure, surprise me." She faced her fear that if she didn't organise everything it wouldn't happen. Her birthday came and she was very happily surprised!

Esther also had a secret wish to do a totally different job, a wish she'd had for many years. I was the first person she ever told about it and she expected me to laugh at her. I didn't laugh. I was excited and the very next session, we worked on a resume and I encouraged her to apply for advertised positions in that exact job. She was interviewed by two major companies and offered two jobs and got to choose the company that she felt had the better reputation. Over time, with her homework, she expressed all kinds of things to her husband and he was her biggest supporter as her life became an empowered version of what she wanted. Forwarding the clock to now, Esther and her husband co-manage their finances, overseas holidays and all other family and social activities—they are a team—and guess what . . . her husband was fantastically relieved to not have to do it all alone.

Esther got all that she wanted when she engaged her free will and got support to feel differently about herself, her life, her options and her own power.

I also have a lot of clients who talk to loved ones who have passed over, or to their angels and guides and other spiritual helpers. This, by the way, is an incredibly powerful resource to utilise if it is in alignment with your belief system.

However, no angel or guide or spiritual helper of any kind can interfere with free will—it is your birth right to live and learn in your own way and at your own pace this lifetime. They are there to help and guide, with love and compassion but not to choose *for* you.

Go back for a moment and check in on Day 16 again, the day about your *blurk* and how to get out of it. There are often times where, on some level of our being we are choosing, with our free will, to stay disconnected from financial abundance or stay in fear of totally opening up to our power. Your angels and guides (if you believe in those) cannot directly interfere with something you are choosing, which is why this book began with all the information about your thinking and mindset programming. It is very important to understand the how, the structure of why you are where you are and why you have been where you have been. What thinking is getting in the way of opening you up to manifesting what you want? You have the power to manifest your dream life and you're using that power every day whether you are aware of it or not. Once your thoughts and mindset programming are aligned with what you want to create, then your angels, guides and passed-over loved ones are there to step in as an invisible support team, silent partners to your success in every area of life. Until then, they are probably guiding you to books like this, health practitioners, people who have experienced and triumphed over your current issues (or who are still stuck there but in listening to them, the answer of what to do becomes obvious giving you the opportunity to apply the learning to your own situation). This is what your support team does.

Get into *cause* and out of *effect* and know that other people, angels, guides and any spiritual help is only able to be helping you to the point that you allow.

Remember too, that your body is the vehicle through which you receive your help. If you've just had 16 buckets of drugs or alcohol and you're asking your angels to manifest you a fabulous new partner who is rich, healthy and lives a clean lifestyle, how do you think they can go about arranging this? Perhaps the first thing you might be attracted to is a book like this. That's your guidance giving you step one.

What action are you taking to receive the experience you're wanting? One of my favourite sayings of all time is, "God doesn't home deliver." I once lived with someone called Sarah who had been out of work for some time. When people asked how the job hunting was going she would readily respond by saying, "Oh it's so hard/there's not much out there/everyone wants you to have experience," which were believable lines to the listener. In reality, Sarah had decided that after a decade of experience in one industry, she wanted to change direction and had crafted a beautiful affirmation about her perfect job but had taken no action what-so-ever to decide what her new area of interest was. She stayed unemployed. She never looked through TAFE or university booklets or researched other industries but instead affirmed that she had the perfect job. Sarah very rarely socialised, watched a lot of television and led a very sedentary lifestyle. She was a perfect vibrational match for the industry she'd worked in for over 10 years, but would never respond to those advertisements in the newspaper because she thought it was time for a change and simultaneously took no action to apply for new work or to find a new interest or industry.

Did the dream job not get delivered mysteriously one day because affirmations don't work?

Really, is that what any part of you thinks?

Or did the dream job not get delivered because no one with the dream job knew Sarah existed.

Creating new things in your life requires newness. You need to be the instigator of that newness. So out of the blame game and into your power we continue to go.

Today's Commitment to Authentic Personal Power

Answer these questions for yourself right now:

What is something I can do today that will move me in the direction of my dreams or realising what my dreams are?

If I were to continually ask this question every day for the next month and take the action that springs to mind . . . what would happen?

How would I feel about myself and my life as a direct result of taking these actions?

"I happily do what it takes to realise my dreams
I find that action really easy"
Lyrics from, "Positively Funky—Affirmations for Anybody,
Anytime & Anywhere" *Track:* I happily do.

https://itunes.apple.com/au/artist/iesha-delune/id501840701

DAY 23

Lifting Your Vibration Part 1

Ways of being

There are many thoughts, feelings and actions that constrict or expand your energy and today we're going to talk about some of these. Scattered throughout this book are many more examples. In the coming days we will be talking about that fantastically clever body of yours and its role in your uplifted energy and ongoing personal empowerment. Today is about noticing some common patterns, the impact they have and how easy it is to transform your energy.

Believe you are powerful

We have already talked about the power of your mind and the positive mental benefits of being at *cause*. Think now about the energetic outcomes of being at *cause* and at *effect* . . . What does feeling a victim of external circumstances do to your energy levels? What does knowing you have the power to change things for the better do to your energy levels? By using the unhealed past as your reference point, you can only imagine more and more of the same. Understanding that you are a dynamic, creative being in a constant state of healing, repair, growth and change opens your perspective to imagine new, improved and joyous circumstances. The very first time you step wholly into *cause* and accept yourself as the powerful being you are (and every time after that first time) you open your energy and feel the freedom you truly have.

Stop being a human chameleon and allow people to know and love *You*

Have you ever said "yes" when you wished to say "no"?
Have you ever said "no" when you wished to be saying "yes"?

What have those experiences been like energetically?

By learning to communicate clearly and setting healthy boundaries you can start to be your beautiful, individual self. It is normal to feel you need support in achieving this. I can't count the number of clients I've worked with who, initially, thought their whole world would crumble if they were to express truthfully to the people around them about the way they feel. What do you think their energy was like, living daily with such a profound denial of self? When a loved one said, "I love you," do you think they were able to accept that in as a genuine connection? When you show the people around you the mask you think they want you to be wearing, rather than sharing the truth, it constricts your energy. As you feel the freedom that is truly yours and allow yourself, in that space, to be vulnerable and powerful and share your truths you can know true love and connection. This will expand your energy.

Denying and repressing your feelings stagnates your energy. Working through and expressing your feelings, expands your energy and creates freedom and flow (and all the positive benefits that come with that).

Expressing yourself honours not only you but also everyone around you and the end result is something beautiful.

Live in accordance with your values

Think about the best workplace you've been in . . . what made it great? Generally when company values match your own, and those values are infused through management and the organisation's culture, it is a pleasure to go to work. Working in a role that you personally value really helps, too.

In my travelling years I had many and varied jobs with a huge variety of workplaces and I still remember the horrible, constricted energy of walking into a workplace that didn't match my values (and this was before I even understood values at the unconscious level).

As an example, let's imagine person a) values community living and shared resources and person b) values the power of each individual to create fantastic circumstances for themselves. There is no one truth for everyone, which is why person a) and person b) would be happy in very different careers and life circumstances.

It is possible to happily co-exist in beautiful partnerships and other close relationships with people who don't have the exact same values but not if, by doing so, you compromise your own.

You'll know when your values are compromised by how it feels.

What would you like to do about that from now on?

Do what you say you're going to do

Knowing that you're the kind of person who does what they say they're going to do (even when the commitment has been made in the privacy of your own mind) builds self-esteem. Breaking commitments that you've made to yourself or to others that you care about feels a lot less nice.

I would like to make the point here that change is also totally fine. There is a difference between breaking a commitment to yourself and changing strategies in order to achieve your goals. For example, if you had a goal to get fit, you may start by joining a gym with a commitment to yourself to go three times a week. Signing up, going a few times and never again is breaking a commitment to you and will have an energy-lowering effect. However, going to the gym a few times and realising it's not really your thing is different. From this place you can look for a replacement activity that will still accomplish your exercise-three-times-a-week goal. You might go to a martial arts class and totally love it and end up exercising more than three times a week because you've found your thing. In this way, you've kept the energy of your goal alive while using the process of trial and correction to make the necessary adjustments for maximum 'enjoyablilty'.

Use your imagination for the power of positivity

We all have an imagination and use it every single time we are thinking about the future. If you're going to play make believe inside your mind about stuff that hasn't even happened then why not imagine something fabulous?

There are times in adult life when we need to be assessing and thinking of the future. If you're finding the process of applying for a home loan a bit stressful, thinking about all the future repayments, I'm not suggesting that you imagine winning the lottery, having that taking care of it all and then apply for the loan based on that unpredictable plan. However, if you are applying for a home loan that you can currently afford and find yourself imagining other unlikely realities like, "What if I lose my job and can't find another one ever?" or "What if my partner dies, how will I afford it then?" or "What if I lose my leg in an horrific truck accident?" then you may as well imagine fantastic things happening instead of all that unsubstantiated, horrible stuff. Which kind of imagining is going to make you feel better?

If there is a promotion available at work, who is more likely to get it? The person who has insurance policies out for every imaginable outcome due to intense fear of life itself or the person who is happy, confident and motivated to have new experiences? This confidant person may also have insurances by the way, but other than paying the bill, it's not in their mind—they're too busy experiencing new experiences, learning, growing and living.

You create feelings and also intense hormonal reactions with your imagination, so use it wisely—which means use it mostly to create fun, enjoyable imaginings and you will benefit energetically, physically and mentally.

Use your ability to speak for the power of positivity

How often do you use your words to say negative things about yourself and about other people? Gossip can be very damaging in a practical way for the people involved but energetically it's like drinking lead—heavy and *blurk*-generating.

I am a fan of Socrates' Triple Filter Test:

He said that before telling him something you should take a moment to filter what you're going to say by checking:

1)   Are you absolutely sure that what you are about to share is true?
2)   Is it kind? Is it good?
3)   Is it useful?

I'd also be adding in: Is it something that you would like to be said about you?

Would the kinds of things you say about yourself and others change dramatically if you used these filters in your daily life? Would your humorous comments in conversations with other people change much? Would some of your relationships change?

Try doing this for a single day and see what, if anything needs to change if you're following these four filters. Then notice what those changes do for you energetically . . . you may be very surprised at the grounded expansion and self-esteem that comes when you utilise these filters as 'rules' for life.

It is completely OK to get support in your relationships by talking with other people. Just be aware of how you run that conversation. There is a huge difference between spending half an hour saying how terrible someone is and spending half an hour asking for support for how to better manage yourself in specific situations. Energetically the first is disempowering and therefore energy-lowering and the second one is empowering and therefore lifts your energy.

Keeping stuff clean and organised

I really admire those people who seem to always have neat and clean houses, cars and desks. To be honest, I've never been one of them. What I have come to experience though is the difference it makes having things clean and organised so I make time to make it happen, rather than it being a naturally-generated priority. Think of the energetic quality of gliding (I have wooden floor boards and am often wearing socks) into your office to use some sticky tape, using it and going on to the next task versus gliding into your office to use some sticky tape, not having any idea where it is, making a mess looking for it, then having to clean that mess up (or not—just leave it there) and going on to the next task. Can you feel the difference, just reading those two scenarios? Being at *cause* practically means things like managing your health and being up to date with your finances, taxation and book keeping. Knowing where things are and knowing where things are at in your life creates lightness. Not knowing where and how things are creates stagnation energetically and causes stresses and negative imaginings.

Open channels to manifest your goals

One of the greatest energetic anti-depressants is taking action.

In Day 22, I shared a story about Sarah. She had very low, stagnant energy due to lack of exercise, diet and a general it's-all-so-hard attitude. The longer she stayed unemployed the later she would stay up at night, the longer she would sleep in, the more alcohol and junk food she'd consume. She did a lot of thinking about where her life had gone wrong, the people who hadn't loved her enough and blaming the outside world for her current circumstances. She was spending savings rather than adding to savings, eventually, once the savings were spent, she was living on credit and her energy was getting more and more depressed.

Choosing to open channels for a new job to arrive would have had an instant, positive impact on her. Socialising with friends and talking with new people would have opened up the number of people who knew her and knew she was looking for work. Stepping into *cause* would have gotten things moving and created changes that would lead to more positive changes. In the end, that is exactly what happened. She took a low-income job that required physical activity just to get things moving, which put her in a mindset to contact someone she hadn't spoken to since being unemployed which lead to her being employed in a matter of weeks. Our paths still cross and she's happily working, living in a great relationship and working towards her next goals.

The purpose of these stories is *never* to judge. Most of us have experienced highs and lows in life. In fact, if you've never had a low, how can you even comprehend that the high is a high? For me, it is in the lowest of the lows that I have learned the most about myself and as a direct result made the most powerful, life-changing decisions. I couldn't be where I am now if I hadn't had the wheels fall off and sat in a dark *blurk* the number of times that I have. If you were in a place like that when you started this book then know you have already shifted energetically into a more expanded, lighter place. Just taking one step, one action, will ease the way forward to the next step and next action on the road to happiness. Most of my clients who've been in that hopeless, dark place now take deliberate care of themselves, energetically, mentally, and physically as part of their inspiration to never head back there and as part of enjoying their renewed vigour and appreciation for life. These tools you're learning are practical ways for you to run your innate equipment for life—they're with you all the time, you're creating your life experiences using them, they're totally free and it is pretty easy to create change in just one area to deliberately uplift the rest.

Taking action towards your goals 'gets the ball rolling' and it's only once it is in motion that you can see where it's going, what the next step needs to be and where to make adjustments. Don't rob yourself of the fantastic life experience of achieving your goals and stretching further to the next ones.

If you want support with setting goals (the kind that you'll definitely take action to achieve) then check out my free e-book, "How to Set Goals You'll Achieve—a fabulous resource for making life amazing" at *www.wholisticvitality.com.au*.

Today's Commitment to Authentic Personal Power

* A note about personal commitments: While I can look back on my life and see the big decisions and major turning points, the daily action required was often very small. It is OK to make a big decision and take small, incremental steps towards your goal—in fact, it is often more sustainable that way rather than radical shifts. Either way is fine but just look back and see what has worked for you in the past. Use this book, and the rest of your life, as an opportunity to really get to know and appreciate yourself, your values and what works for you. If major, over-night transformations have been the way you've achieved things in your past then stick with that. If that method has left you crashing and burning, feeling bad about yourself or with a whole lot of changes begun but never finished, then perhaps you're more of a slow-and-steady-wins-the-race kind of being. Both are great, both work, but they just work differently for different people.

Pick one of the patterns above that has been an issue for you and spend some time thinking over that pattern in your life then ask yourself the questions below.

Where am I now with regards to this pattern?

Where would I like to be?

How has being that old way affected my energy and vitality for life?

When I am where I would like to be, how will that affect my energy and vitality for life?

What can I commit to today that will begin to bring about that transformation?

DAY 24

Lifting Your Vibration Part 2

Things to do

Today I'm going to quickly share six of the ways you can lift your energy to access all that better-feeling stuff already within yourself. I'm going to share six easy things to do in order to feel instantly better and build a better-feeling vibration over time as well.

Let me be extremely clear, the ideas shared today are merely suggestions for things to try. You may already know about these ideas and practices, but it never hurts to be reminded of your existing wisdom. We all forget to use the tools we have sometimes. Since my first mobile phone, I have used the alarm or reminder system to remember to do the things that serve me (like some of the things listed today). Please don't think that you have to incorporate each and every one of these tools into your weekly life, or you'll end up a frazzled mess (which incidentally will lower your vibration). My intention is that you complete this book with a collection of answers so that you can always pull one out of your hat and magically improve your 'now'.

There are also many days to come that refer to other methods of lifting your vibration including topics such as at conscious breathing, dietary choices, exercise, uplifting people, and enjoying your sensuality.

Low, slow, heavy, *blurky* vibration can only exist where there is no energetic flow. In essence all of the suggestions today, and throughout the entire book, are based around knowing firstly that *you* are in charge of you and secondly that change creates change. Each of the three areas—mind, energy, and body all work together. Even if you positively impact just one of these areas you will positively affect the other components too. Days 35, 36, and 37 will deal with this directly, but it is beneficial to familiarise yourself with the idea now. For example, going for a walk doesn't just make your body feel better because you're getting exercise and breathing more deeply. It also gets your energy moving, releasing stagnation, and with that upliftment you will naturally access the better-feeling thoughts you have in your program.

Meditation

Meditation has been practiced for thousands of years as a tool for connecting with the self and connection with universal oneness. Just like de-fragging your computer frees up space on your hard-drive, meditation supports mental hygiene, clarity, and peace of mind. Whether you're into the idea of universal oneness or not, meditation is well known for its de-stressing properties. A regular practice will cultivate inner strength, enhance concentration, improve the ability to relax (during the day and for sleeping), and encourage healing on all levels of your being.

If you have the skill to mediate, are you using it regularly?

If you've always wanted to learn, what's stopping you? There are lots of free programs with reputable teachers on the internet and probably printed or audio resources at your local library if you'd rather spend your money on other things.

Get outside

I had a lovely picture up on my wall for quite a while that showed a tent pitched in the wilderness. The tent was surrounded by mountains, huge green trees, a river flowing past, and a waterfall in the distance. The caption on the picture read:

Think outside.
No box required.

It was there to remind me that, even in the winter, it is so momentous to get outside and breathe fresh air. Just remembering that picture now makes me take a deep breath and imagine being in a place like that—I can feel the energetic benefits and I'm only making pictures inside my head. Nature has a balance and vitality that is deeply enriching for your energy field.

How often do you spend time outside?

How could you incorporate a bit more outside time into your life?

Space clearing

Clearing out clutter, destructive behaviours, and people from your life are delightful energetic gifts to give yourself.

Clutter

Have you ever visited someone whose house is packed to the brim with piles of disorganised stuff? Or can your home get a bit that way? How does it feel to be in places like that? How does it feel to be in a home or car that is clean and organised?

I'm all for being a collector of 'stuff' but it needs to be organised in such a way that it is easy to find and clean around—otherwise this stuff will create stagnation and inhibit your energy flow. Knowing where things are saves time and alleviates annoyance. It also reduces negative internal dialog (if you're like most people who apologise to visitors for the state of their home or car, indicating that they must care about it on some level).

Have you ever done a massive spring clean (regardless of the season)? I don't know about you, but when I sort out my children's' cupboards and get rid of clothes that are too small, it makes me feel as though I've lost weight. I cleaned out my refrigerator recently and afterwards I felt as if I'd won some money. Clarity of stuff creates clarity in your vibrational field also.

If there's a part of your house that you avoid thinking about, then I suggest taking the time to tackle it for the purpose of losing some energetic weight. You'll feel fabulous. If your whole home feels a bit that way, then just take it one room at a time and soon you'll love being in every room.

Behaviours

If you do or say something you feel a bit guilty about you are creating stagnation in your system. Even if you are exceptionally good at putting on a big bravado about how you're totally comfortable being exactly how you are. Generally, people who are actually comfortable with something do not even mention it at all—unless it's new. For example, if you get a new hair cut that you like, you may mention it as you see people for the first time, but if something that feels outlandish and you're not 100% comfortable with it, you might keep on speaking about it to justify your choice.

You may also have some habits that you'd prefer not to have. In these cases, you are often creating heaviness in your energy—a bit like I mentioned in Day 23. Some part of you has to be aware that you're living out of alignment with your values.

If this is true for you, then why not choose today to kick one of those habits? If it's a biggie, then look around for the right support. You'll feel energetically uplifted as more and more of your behaviour matches your vision of the best version of yourself.

People

There are always people who bring out the best in you and people who bring out the stuff that you know is not your finest. You get to choose how intimately you connect with all of the kinds of people in your life. There are always ways to step into the positive and back a little (or the whole way out of) the negative influences in your life.

How often are you able to say "no" to any negative influences in your life?

How often do you make the effort to connect with the people you feel bring out your best? Can you make contact with one of them today?

Money and savings

Having the deep and secure unconscious knowing that you are financially safe and that everything is going to be ok is a wonderfully practical method of raising your vibration. Having money to meet your basic living costs and to more-than-cover your spending allows you to unconsciously relax. This lifts your vibration and you can focus on other things like inspiration in your work or other money-making endeavours.

Depending on your current financial situation, this may seem like a long-term goal. Regardless of how things are 'now' the main point is to get into *cause* and have clarity about your circumstances. Whenever we choose to avoid something that we imagine might be uncomfortable, we are creating stagnation energetically. We are also living fully at the effect of something we don't even have the details about.

I have a client who is about to open her second business due to the success of her first, but when she first came to me a few years ago, she was suppressing a whole lot of anxiety about her finances. She hadn't done an income tax return for five years and she felt that she'd earned a lot but didn't know how much. She hadn't paid any tax and was very frightened about what would happen when she finally 'fessed up'.

What do you think her energy was like when that topic came up? There was fear of the amounts of money involved and self-judgment about, "Doing the wrong thing." She didn't have any facts, but she would oscillate between suppressing it all (pretending everything was OK) and by blowing things out of proportion (thinking of astronomical fines and tax amounts).

Imagine carrying that around for five years? Her energy shifted as soon as she hired a data entry person to input all her paperwork. It continued to shift in a truly positive direction as the boxes where she stored her financial information, invoices, and receipts got smaller. She was so much lighter once it was all sorted out and she proudly got her tax done and arrived in the now. In every financial situation, you are much better off dealing with facts and making a plan to help you achieve your financial goals. Choosing to bury your head in the sand creates energetic stagnation. Taking your head out of the sand will get you into *cause* and empower you to create a new 'now'—perhaps sooner than you think.

If there's anything in your financial life that you've been avoiding, then today is the day to get clear and empowered with a plan.

Digest before sleeping

I've learned many incredible, energy raising, and empowering things from one of my best friends who is a practitioner of Ayurvedic medicine. From her suggestions, I have incorporated a few lifestyle changes that have made an immense vibrational difference. One of these is not eating within three hours of going to bed. Now, on the occasions that I am unable to keep with this intention, I wake up feeling like I've got a hangover (without the alcohol that would generally precede such a feeling) and it takes me a lot longer to get up and about. It is such a basic tool to add to your life, and I just had to share it. The three hours is specific to me and is dependent on how fast your body digests food. If you have slow digestion, then more than three hours are necessary. The idea is not to be sleeping and digesting at the same time.

Experiment for yourself with various timeframes and see how you feel in the morning (mentally, physically, and energetically) when you've given your body time to digest before going to sleep.

Pure, organic essential oils

These oils will instantly affect energetic changes. Using them is a science unto itself but there is a lot of information about what oil to use for what conditions and desired emotional states. With the right quality of oil, just inhaling the essence will create change. I use organic essential oils daily for myself and in sessions with clients, and I find they enhance healing in a very powerful way.

Here is a quick list of all the things we've talked about in previous days that lift vibration:

- Getting out of *effect* and into *cause*
- Expressing yourself
- Choosing new beliefs
- Being in the now
- Changing your perspective to something more positive
- Positive affirmations
- Releasing the need to keep playing the guilt-program
- Shifting perceptions to more empowering and resourced ones
- Understanding (and therefore, not suppressing) your *blurk* and moving through it
- Wanting something and making a plan to make it happen

Today's Commitment to Authentic Personal Power

Today is about taking some action, so choose an activity to raise your vibration.

Notice how you feel before, during, and afterwards.

DAY 25

The Role of Your Physical Body

An introduction to what your
physical vehicle needs to run optimally

Take just a moment to look at your physical being . . .

What thoughts and judgments do you have about your body?

How do these thoughts make you feel?

How well do you actually know your body and what its needs are?

Do you listen when your body tells you basic things like, "I'm hungry," or "I'm full'" or "Please rest my ankle or you'll do more damage to it," "I'm tired," or "Get up and out and get moving, I need exercise," "I'm uncomfortable, please shift positions?" How about: "I really don't like that person, can we please not spend time with them?"

Your body is your vehicle for moving around in your life. Like any vehicle, it requires maintenance or it breaks down. Maintenance for your magical, physical body falls into three categories—physical, mental and vibrational, which is wonderful because you always have so many ways to feel physically better!

Your physical body, like everything else in the Universe is in a constant state of change. Every second of every day it is rebuilding itself. The body that you just looked at, didn't exist two years ago, all those old cells have died and have been replaced. How exciting is that? When I'm teaching, I like to look out at the smiling and empowered faces and think about all the happy cells they're making, because in every moment, we can change our lives and build a stronger, healthier body.

Our bodies are designed to be happy. By that I mean, a great mental attitude is a really significant ingredient for your body to do what it is designed to do, as efficiently as it can.

In stark contrast, a down, dark, ugly mental attitude, mean-to-yourself internal dialogue, and stress can put a whole lot of strain on our bodies and use up resources that could be used for the constant repair and maintenance that's going on at a microscopic level. So, using the tools you've already learned to run your brain in a way that makes good feelings, is a magnificent gift you can give your physical vehicle.

Our bodies also perform their best work with free-flowing energy moving throughout the various energy systems we have.

Today we're going to get specific about the 'physical' needs your body has to be the best vehicle it can possibly be. You need your body in order to get around, living a fabulous life, so why not make it as healthy as it can be so you can be here, living and learning, experiencing and loving for as long as possible?

Movement and exercise—This is not the part where I tell you that you have to go out and buy a Lycra outfit. It's where I remind you that your parts need to be used. In some cases it's the, "use it or lose it" scenario, like with your physical flexibility. In other cases, like with your lungs, if you only breathe in a fast and shallow way, not allowing all of your lungs to fill with deep, full breaths, you create toxicity and stress in your body. Your body is designed to move—how often do you prioritise that?

Rest and sleep—You've read the above, you know about moving your parts. You don't, however, need to be doing this all the time. You can over-do the movement and exercise at the expense of rest and quality sleep and this is not a good thing. Physical downtime to recharge your system is vital for your health. Over the years I have helped a lot of clients who have struggled to relax and get the hours of sleep they need. The physical transformations are quite astounding when someone goes from restless to rested. The mental and emotional transformations that follow being rested are amazing as well. How much peace do you create in your life? How many nights a week do you have uninterrupted, rejuvenating sleep?

Quality Food—In the wild spectrum of possibilities when it comes to food, I've worked with clients who range from intensely micro-managing every gram of every ingredient that goes into their mouth to clients who have never once considered the quality or ingredients in their food. Where do you sit on the spectrum? Where would you like to sit?

Senses pleasantly stimulated—My senses are featured frequently in the daily gratitude journal that I keep. How amazing is it to live in a vehicle that can see, hear, feel, smell, taste and sense energy like our bodies can? Have you ever thought that maybe senses need exercise too? In the case of your eyesight, it's actually really important for your brain to use your range of vision i.e. look at things up close and far away. Likewise, pleasure is crucial for vitality. Put simply, using and delighting your senses creates positive chemical responses in your system. Smelling a delicious meal before eating it aids digestion. Listening to classical music stimulates the neurons in your brain. Massaging your skin with warmed oil stimulates and invigorates, nourishes and detoxifies all levels of your being.

We are going to go into all of these areas separately in the days to come. For today, I just wanted to introduce the areas we'll be covering and get you thinking about your "magical" body in a new way.

How often do you take stock of all of your body's achievements? It's like you have a factory with millions of staff working hard each and every minute of the day to produce what you see when you look at yourself. All of those cells, your loyal staff, can only work with the ingredients you provide and in the working conditions you provide. How stressed are they? How happy and relaxed are they? Are there positive messages coming out over the loud speaker (your internal dialogue) or are there you're-just-not-good-enough messages being played while they're there working so hard for you. Whatever working conditions you're providing, your body continues to do the best work it possibly can—what an amazing gift!

If you've ever been seriously ill, you will probably have a whole new appreciation of how magical it feels to be healthy. If you've ever had a debilitating physical condition, you will probably have experienced the simple joy of being able to move again after the healing is complete. When you've been sick, do you take the time to celebrate your clever body for getting you well again? The effort that goes into maintaining something as simple as body temperature is quite remarkable. You can see these words because your remarkable body is keeping track of how moist your eyeballs are and blinking to keep the moisture level optimum. Your unconscious mind has now made you aware of how often you're blinking, but as soon as you move on and fill those plug holes of conscious awareness with new cords of information, you can stop paying attention to how often you're blinking and trust your talented body to take care of that on your behalf.

How often do you say, "Thank you" to your body for your life—nothing you've ever experienced, ever, would have been possible without it.

Think about that . . .

The whole point of bringing all these areas to your attention is for you to have a long list of things you can do, right now, to feel better. By feeling better, right now, you will be more attracted to doing other things that match with your better feeling. You can start anywhere. When you choose better quality food you're more inclined to go for a walk after dinner. When you go for a walk before a meal, you're more inclined to eat something with a higher vibration because you're energy is higher. You get to choose the starting point for getting the ball rolling on feeling better.

Today's Commitment to Authentic Personal Power

Part 1: Your "magical" body is a sensational machine, filled and covered with receptors to accept data from the world around you and within you so that it can respond and make changes where necessary. Are you listening to the feedback?

Today, where possible, I want for you to pay special attention to your physical body. What's it saying to you? Is it giving you feedback that it's comfortable or not? Is it letting you know it's hungry, or not? Does it feel like moving or resting? How do you respond to your body's needs?

Part 2: Think back over your entire life and make a list of the top eleven things that you love and appreciate your body for:

1)

2)

3)

4)

5)

6)

7)

8)

9)

10)

11)

And keep right on going, if you're on a roll!! Just think of how good it makes your "staff" feel when they are acknowledged for all their hard work!

Before going on to Day 26, take some time to reflect about your day of paying attention to your body. Were you more aware of the feedback you were getting? When you got some feedback, did you ignore your body's needs or instinctively listen and make adjustments?

DAY 26

The Power of Breath Part 1

What breathing can do (other than just keeping you alive)
Introduction to Square Breathing

I breathe in life . . . I breathe out peace

Take a deep breath in through your nose . . . and slowly breathe it out though your mouth.

Now continue using just your nose to breathe in . . . and out . . . slowly and deeply . . . making the inflow and outflow of your breaths as long as you comfortably can.

Take one minute out of your day, right now, to just repeat that process. Breathing in . . . through your nose . . . and gently out . . . through your nose . . . paying attention to what parts of your body move when you take in big, deep breaths . . . and what parts of your body surrender and relax as you breathe out.

You have just learned one of the most valuable tools in this book: conscious breathing. You know that you can trust your unconscious mind to take care of breathing for you without you having to pay attention. Conscious breathing is when you choose to take charge and breathe with focused attention.

The first thing that conscious breathing does is make you present in the now—getting you out of your head and giving you space to connect with yourself and your resources. In a stressful space, breathing buys you time. It actually gives you a moment to create space just for you. It enhances rest and relaxation throughout your time awake and will also improve the quality of your sleep. It allows you to be at peace with yourself; not making negative thoughts and feelings. It allows you to connect with your beautiful self. It is one of the easiest ways to awaken the movement out of *effect* and into *cause*—that powerful place where you can choose to create change. In fact, the moment you *choose* to breathe consciously, you have arrived at *cause* because you realise you are in control of the present moment.

In many ancient traditions, like yoga and qi gong, it is taught that if you can regulate your breath then you can control your mind. I totally agree with them based on my own experiences and the transformations I have seen in clients and students. Think back to the librarian of your unconscious mind. What an amazing resource you have there. This is an example of how things are meant to be—your mind being supportive of you. The powerhouse that is your amazing mind is a resource that is meant to be supportive of you, not controlling of you, and your breath is the quickest way to harness the mind so that it works for you rather than against you. Conscious breathing brings you into the now—the only time where change can actually take place i.e. you cannot think your way into changing the past or the future, but what you choose to do now can positively reframe the past and create a more joyous future. 'Now' is where you need to be in order to be authentically and personally powerful and conscious breathing brings you straight there.

Deep, conscious breathing also enhances all of your body's functions. It super oxygenates every system allowing them and all of your organs to function at a higher level. For this reason it is not uncommon for people with a regular conscious breathing practice to get sick less than those who don't. Let me put it this way: restricted breathing greatly compromises your overall health, vitality and ability to think clearly. By practicing the art of conscious breathing you can create magical transformations on all levels of yourself. You can nourish your whole body with increased oxygen and expulsion of carbon dioxide. You will also reduce stress hormones, calm your emotions, massage your heart and abdominal organs, aid detoxification and relax your muscles. Put simply, your body will function more efficiently which means more fuel in your energetic tank for health and vitality.

All levels of your being are cleansed through conscious breathing—the physical, mental, emotional and energetic.

How did you go with Day 25, paying attention to your body's needs? If you felt disconnected from your body then today will be transformational for you. Breathing is, quite simply, your greatest asset for uplifting every area of your life. By giving your breathing even just one plug of conscious awareness you increase your body's resources. With each breath you are breathing in oxygen, a vital ingredient for all body processes. With each breath you are also breathing in life-force energy and activating your own energetic upliftment.

Square Breathing

The counts can be as long or as short as you need them to be to easily breathe in this square formation as comfortably and evenly as your normal breathing. Like any skill, this breathing technique will take some time to master. The more you practise, the more your breathing will easily flow and this exercise will leave you feeling connected to that awesome body of yours and to the positivity that already exists inside you. If you find that you are feeling dizzy or light-headed then immediately shorten the count of each breath. Generally, most people find the in-breath and the first hold easy. It is quite normal to then find the out-breath and second hold more challenging. Base your counts on how much breath you have left for the out-breath and hold stages or whichever stage you find the most challenging. The purpose is the evenness of the square; not breathing as big and long as you can. Once all of the sides are even, you can lengthen each of the counts as long as each phase is the same length.

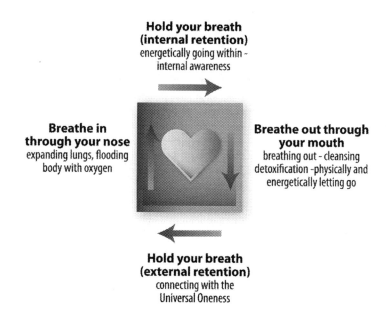

**Hold your breath
(internal retention)**
energetically going within -
internal awareness

**Breathe in
through your nose**
expanding lungs, flooding
body with oxygen

**Breathe out through
your mouth**
breathing out - cleansing
detoxification -physically and
energetically letting go

**Hold your breath
(external retention)**
connecting with the
Universal Oneness

Breathing out through your mouth in this exercise is for cleansing, but the optimum breathing for daily life is in and out through the nose.

This is my broad-spectrum, feel-connected-to-myself-and-all-my-resources technique that I've used since learning it in the late 1990s. I believe it to be what saved me from utter lunacy during years of baby-induced sleep deprivation. I use it to increase vitality if I am feeling ill for any reason. I use it to relax my mind if sleep isn't coming easily. I use it to connect with the wisdom of my heart if I am upset about something and need to connect with the truth of it (and stop connecting with everything else in my unconscious mind that matches the upset). Once you put the time in to master the evenness required, it is so simple and easy to practise; it's free and you've got the necessary body parts with you every moment of every day.

Today's Commitment to Authentic Personal Power

1) Breathe with conscious awareness for as much of the next 24 hours as possible. Have the mindfulness of your breath bringing you into the present moment and notice all the positive benefits that result.

2) At any point during the day, set aside fifteen minutes to experiment with and experience the square breathing exercise taught today. Use the first five minutes to establish what speed you will be breathing and allow ten minutes for the practice itself.

Before going on to Day 27, take the time to reflect on your day of conscious breathing.

What were some of the benefits you noticed mentally, physically and energetically?

The Power of Breath Part 2

*The positive effects of breathing—continued
Introduction to alternate nostril breathing*

For those of you who are new to conscious breathing practices I am not expecting an instant 'WOW'. This is more like the over-time 'WOW' that comes from a physical exercise practice or a dietary change practice. Please put the time in though (even if it's only a few minutes a day) to a breathing practice of some kind. You will most definitely feel more alive and spend more of your time at *cause*, which as you know, is the place to be.

Today we are going to talk about and experience alternate nostril breathing, called Nadi Shodhana Pranayama in the yogic tradition. This technique is soothing, unites the left thinking brain with the right feeling brain and calms the central nervous system. It will kick into action your parasympathetic nervous system, which is the branch of your Autonomic Nervous System responsible for your body's ability to recuperate and return to a balanced state of relaxation and renewal after experiencing pain or stress. It is a restorative and balancing breath—far more balancing than your regular breathing—and will support all of the other bodily systems to function properly.

Stress is a toxic state you create within your systems—making them all out of balance. Other breathing techniques allow those systems to function more efficiently. This breathing technique will bring all body systems back into balance—I'm talking here about things like your hormonal system, central nervous system and respiratory systems. If I was going to write another book on this topic, we could break down what each of these systems do in the body to further 'WOW' you as to the impact of this and other breathing techniques, but this book is more of an introduction to your innate resources and for now I heartily recommend that you practice what you learn and reap the immediate and long-term benefits.

Alternate nostril breathing

Sit upright for this exercise and relax your shoulders. If you are comfortable in a folded legs meditation position then sit in this way. Otherwise, sit in a chair with a straight back or against a wall with your feet outstretched so you are comfortably upright.

1: Using your right hand, close off your right nostril with your thumb and inhale slowly through your left nostril.
Support your elbow with your left hand, taking care not to restrict the chest. Alternatively, rest your right elbow on pillows or a table-top or desk that you are sitting next to. The idea is to be comfortable so you can focus on this practice.

2: Using your ring finger of the same hand, slowly close the left nostril and exhale slowly through your right nostril

3: Keeping your ring finger in place, inhale through right nostril

4: Gently close the right nostril (once again with the thumb) and exhale slowly through your left nostril

This is one cycle.

Repeat from step 1.

Start slowly with four cycles and gradually increase. Make sure you take the time to sit quietly for a few moments after you have finished.

For balance, it is important that the duration of the inflow of breath matches the duration of the outflow of breath. Do not force your breath in any way and take care not to speed up the outflow of breath if you're feeling that your body wants to get back to breathing in again. If you notice any discomfort whatsoever then make both the inflow and the outflow shorter to compensate. You may feel as though you haven't breathed in as deeply as you can, but this is not a beat-your-personal-best-breathing-in-time exercise, it is all about the balance of inwards and outwards and this needs to be your priority.

The best time for this practice is first thing in the morning. That said, work with your existing structure and it is much better to use this practice at any time of day than not to do it at all if you've missed the morning timeslot. If you've had a particularly stressful day, some cycles in the evening is OK too, to kick in your relaxation responses and then move to square breathing or conscious, deep and relaxing breathing. Try to avoid doing this on a full stomach, just the same as with physical exercise, because your digestive system has a job to do and you will be drawing energy away from that.

Today's Commitment to Authentic Personal Power

If you haven't already, while reading through today, I want you to try this breathing technique out. Just to get a feel for how to hold your right hand and get the position of your fingers comfortable.

Then, when you next wake up, try this breathing first thing in the morning. As already stated; start with four cycles. As we move through the following days I would strongly suggest maintaining this practice, in the mornings if possible or just wherever you can fit it in.

Take the time to notice how you feel physically, mentally and energetically before, during and after your practice.

DAY 28

Food—Life force for your being

Paying attention to wholistic nutrition

Why do we eat?

Most people would say that we eat because our bodies need fuel. Many parents tell their children to eat their food so they grow up healthy and strong. So often these same adults have stopped thinking about growing healthy and strong themselves. As we've already talked about, your body is growing every day. Perhaps it's no longer growing upwards, but it is regenerating itself every moment of every day, and it needs quality ingredients to do its best work, just like it did when you were growing *up*.

Food is made up of physical components—nutritional ingredients (and the not-so nutritional). Every food also has a vibration of its own. When we eat, we are feeding our "factory workers" with the nutritional ingredients they need for optimal maintenance and repair, health and vitality. While eating we are also infusing our energy with the vibration of our food. Have you ever thought of it in that way?

What was your last meal? When you think of the ingredients of that meal, how long ago was it living and growing? How many processes had it been through from the time it left wherever it was and ended up in your mouth? Typically the answers to these questions will give you an idea of how much nutritional and energetic value your meal had.

There are many different philosophies around diet and nutritional requirements for human health. I am not planning to endorse or criticise any of them here. Most philosophies however do agree that the fresher your ingredients, the higher the quality of your meal and therefore, the better the results for your body. Most also agree that if you took a carrot, washed it and ate it there would be more nutrients present than if you took a carrot, washed it, liquefied it, boiled it, froze it for three months, unfroze it, microwaved it and then drank it. Most would agree that the nutrients available in the soil the carrot grew in would have an impact also. The more nutrient rich the soil is, the more nutrient-rich the resulting carrot.

I think of it mostly like this: The more alive my food is, the more alive I am.

'Convenience' food causes a lot of inconvenience for you physically and therefore mentally and energetically.

Have you ever taken the time to notice the difference?

How do you feel after a pre-packaged, processed, made-months-ago microwave meal?

How do you feel after eating a large-chain, mass-produced fast-food meal?

How do you feel after a fresh, healthy meal?

My own relationship with food was heightened dramatically after the birth of my daughter. She had severe allergies to so many things that I had to invest in thoroughly educating myself and being even more of a label reading, ingredient checker than ever before. She has been such a gift to me in that regard because I've learned so much more about food while on the journey of creating health and vitality for her. One of my most startling discoveries has been learning about food additives, labelling laws and the international variations. When I started looking up additives (the numbers on your ingredients label) I was horrified to see that some of the numbers in the food in our supermarkets were banned in other countries due to tests showing they cause asthmatic responses or stomach upsets and other physical problems. Sometimes these numbers would even be in the "Health Food" isle at my supermarket. I strongly recommend the book, *The Chemical Maze* (*http://www.chemicalmaze.com/*). It will teach you about additives in foods and cosmetics—it's horrifying but enlightening and it will guide you in making choices that will build a healthier body.

The more your "factory workers" are trying to eliminate toxins from your body, the less resources they have for maintaining your vitality. Think of it this way:

Toxins= Power-less
Detox= Power-more

With the help of a good natural health practitioner you can clean and clear out your body of old toxins. Whether you launch into doing a specific cleanse or not, you can radically transform your body's vitality by making different food choices, starting from your next meal. Your body is rebuilding itself constantly so the new choices will be building a healthier and happier you right from the moment you start.

Remember, the more alive your food is, the more alive you are.

A note on your state of mind right now: at some level you were already aware of at least some of the things (or perhaps everything) that I've just said about your food. If your last few meals were not so healthy, then right now you might be feeling a bit down on yourself. If that's happening—STOP! How you think is generating how you feel so just stop and focus on this present moment. You have chosen to read a wholistic book about empowering yourself—YAY you! You can add fresher ingredients into your diet from your next meal and that will have a positive effect. Life is long and life is all about learning, so perhaps now, if it feels right for you, it's time to prioritise yourself and put the best ingredients you can afford into that magical body of yours to fuel your wonderful new life.

Thinking now about the food you choose to eat, are you at *cause* or *effect* with it? Assuming you're not a young child or in prison, you have total control over what goes in your mouth. Your choices on a daily basis are building your body for now and for your future. It is an empowering thing to look at yourself, honour your magical body and decide to do your best.

What are you like when you have an important visitor coming over to your house? Do you look around and make sure your place is clean? Well I like to think of it this way: your individual spark of life-force energy is visiting your physical body right now—how clean have you made it?

Also, did you know that your food cravings may be linked to nutritional deficiencies? When I am craving chocolate, but instead drink a magnesium supplement, the craving usually goes away. According to Carol Simontacchi, C.C.N., M.S., "A deficiency in any of five specific minerals and their cofactors may contribute to a craving for high-sugar carbohydrates. These minerals—chromium, magnesium, manganese, vanadium, and zinc—are essential for blood sugar regulation." *http://www.livestrong.com/article/532980-nutritional-deficiency-and-food-cravings/#ixzz2QxCzNVB4*

Today's Commitment to Authentic Personal Power

Part 1: Pay special attention to how you choose your food and notice things like:

Are you always hungry when you eat?

How do you make your choices as to what to eat?

Are you listening to what your body is asking for nutritionally?

And how do you feel during and after eating?

Part 2: Once you are eating, notice your internal dialogue about *what* you are eating. Criticising yourself and your food is a *blurky* thing to do. Once you're eating whatever it is you've chosen, please enjoy it. If it's tasty then enjoy the sensual pleasure of eating something that delights your senses. Your happiness will lighten your energy and allow you to more easily digest your taste sensation. If it's not so tasty then please take the time to imagine the food's aliveness, enlivening your being. Be at *cause* for the choice and find something, or lots of things, to be positive about during your eating experience. This change will be an energetic, mental and physical gift to beautiful 'You'.

DAY 29

Physical Exercise

Supporting wholistic health & vitality with movement

If your body is the physical 'house' for your energetic being, can that energy easily flow around in all the rooms?

So often we are fooled into believing the illusion of our eyesight and thinking of our bodies as solid—and they're not! Your body is made up of 'physical' ingredients, energetic vibration and space . . . wide, open space.

Staying still and not using your body creates energetic, mental and physical stagnation. Moving and exercise creates physical, mental and energetic vitality, too. The system works, beautifully and harmoniously together to create all states of being.

There are two reasons I've included physical exercise in this book. Firstly, it is one of the essential ingredients of radiant health and vitality. Secondly, it can be used as a vibrational uplifting tool to begin the shift out of sticky emotional states and energetic sluggishness. Sometimes it's damned near impossible to shift out of negative thoughts by trying to generate different thoughts that are in opposition to the icky ones. Using your body as the starting point for creating changes allows you a new avenue to positively redirect your thoughts, emotions and energy without challenging them head-on.

Have you ever thought about what physical movement and exercise do wholistically?

Exercise controls weight. Depending on the type and intensity, exercise can help you put weight on, lose weight, maintain weight . . . you get the idea. Physically this is good because being in a healthy weight range reduces stress on your whole system. Mentally this is good because by being healthy you reduce internal judgments that can put a lot of negative pressure on you and your vehicle as a whole (remember that your body works best in the neutral to feeling fabulous range of emotions). Imagine the energetic freedom of living with less stress and more positive internal dialogue. Feels better doesn't it?

Exercise also combats health conditions and diseases. In a whole load of studies the world over, exercising has been shown to prevent or manage a wide range of health problems and concerns. There are thousands of books you can read on this topic. What I want for you to know is that having great blood flow and a healthy, happy immune system has mental and energetic benefits, too. When your immune system succumbs to a serious illness or disease, your physical resources are depleted, leaving you quite tired. Being ill also lowers your energy because your life-force is there adding strength to the healing and repair. Your mental state can also get very sluggish along with your body and vibration. What's great is that the opposite is also true. Health in your body increases your energy and uplifts the thoughts you unconsciously access.

Exercise is also inseparably linked to other areas of wellbeing. People who exercise tend to sleep better. Exercise lifts your vibration and will lead to healthier food choices that match your energy. Quality food also enhances the body's ability to exercise. And moving your body *feels good*!!

One of the other benefits of exercise is building core strength. Core strength is great for posture, reducing back pain and other spinal pressures. I have also seen a direct relationship in myself and in my work between core strength and self-esteem. As a Qi Gong instructor, I have had many students who begin with very poor core strength and very poor self-esteem. It is remarkable to watch how, during practices that build core strength; they slowly make other changes in their lives like setting better boundaries with their children, partners, friends and employers. As you know now, nothing is ever just 'physical' and I acknowledge there are other shifts also happening for those students contributing to every dimension of their wholistic being. What I want for you to know is this: as you build your core strength, you will have more of those days when you're on the verge of a little strutting—self-satisfied in the knowing that everything is going to be not just fine but fabulously more than fine.

As promised on Day 25, I am not suggesting you need to go out and buy a skin-tight jogging outfit if that doesn't match what you're already doing. There are more ways to healthily exercise than there are languages being spoken the world over, so you can definitely find a few that work for you. From there, at least a few times a week, you can choose which one you want to do and viola . . . you get to enjoy the wholistic benefits of exercise.

Today's Commitment to Authentic Personal Power

Exercise!

For a minimum of ten minutes.

Choose an activity that matches your current level of fitness or stretches you just a little bit. This can be anything from some stretches to walking, running or intense weight training—the choice is always yours. If you're reading this and you're home alone with children too young to leave or it's snowing outside then do something inside. There are heaps of core training exercises that require very little space and you probably know some of them already. If you don't have any inside exercise gear like a punching bag or skipping rope then imagine a skipping rope in your hands and skip or imagine a punching bag in front of you and dance about punching it. If you're flat on your back, lying in a hospital bed without the ability to move (I've been there!) then imagine doing the exercise anyway and breathe as if you're doing it right now. There is no reason for anyone not to do this.

And if you are not physically incapacitated but choose to try out the flat-on-your-back-in-hospital visualisation exercise, rather than doing the real thing, do not be surprised when you actually feel more inclined to actually exercise afterwards.

Take a moment to note how you feel, mentally, energetically and physically before, during and the flow-on after-effects of taking this action.

Before:

During:

After:

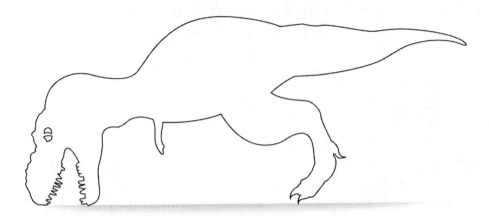

Whatever you choose to do exercise-wise make sure you don't fall victim to the T-Rex syndrome—just because push ups are proving too tricky, doesn't mean that all exercising is too hard and you should give up. There is something that is right for you even if it is as simple as dancing around your lounge room to your favourite songs.

DAY 30

Cause & Effect Part 3

*Making the most of your physical being, regardless of what
you previously considered to be your limitation*

Your body is a magical instrument that is inseparably connected and interwoven with your thoughts and vibration. What you decide to be true about yourself will manifest into your physical reality. Stress kills. Peace and confidence create longevity.

Frowning makes you frown more and access frown-inspiring thoughts. Slouching and breathing shallowly lessens your body's ability to function well, lowers your vibration and allows you to access lower vibrating thoughts. Smiling, even on purpose in the mirror (along with perhaps feeling a little silly) releases happy hormones and opens access to happier thoughts.

Focusing on what you've considered to be your physical limitations, having all the names and terms just right, talking about it, thinking about it, considering how much worse it will get with the passing of time . . . all of these decisions are leading down the path of vibration lowering, immunity lowering physical *blurkiness*.

To illustrate my point, I'll share the stories of two clients with you. A few years ago, I had a couple of clients who were both diagnosed with the same auto-immune disease. The symptoms were varied but included lethargy, nausea and physical aches and pains. Both women were married mothers of young, primary school aged children. How they responded to their medical news couldn't have been more different. One immediately stopped doing anything physical that could possibly aggravate her symptoms—this included everything from exercise to supermarket shopping, working and vacuuming. She came to me feeling almost suicidal with depression. She felt overweight, unhealthy, unattractive and useless. She was always researching how much worse her symptoms could get and had a very dark, bleak view of her future. There were also a lot of problems at home because her husband was working full time and doing most of the jobs at home and living with a very ungrateful, depressed wife who wanted to talk about everything she was missing out on and all the pain she was in all the time. If people didn't feel sorry for her and want to agree with her about the unfair blow life had dealt her, she felt that they just didn't understand what she was going through.

The other client had a very positive attitude. After about a month of down-in-the-dumps and why-me stuff she got proactive and found a naturopath who had a very positive attitude towards managing her symptoms and she found me to support herself mentally and energetically to live as happily and healthily as possible. She researched foods that could help and was actively compliant with all that her naturopath prescribed in the way of supplements and dietary changes. There were days she just had to stay in bed because the pain was too great, but she called these, "The Universe Says It's Time to Rest," days. She used the time on those days, in between sleeping, to read inspiring books and to watch television that made her laugh, or made her think in a new way or just allowed her to escape from her circumstances, rather than focus on them. On those days, if she spoke to anyone, she'd talk about the book she was reading or the show she was watching. She actively avoided anyone, ever feeling sorry for her because she was focused, as often as humanly possible, on all the wonderful things she had in her life rather than the one thing that wasn't going according to plan. As a result, she pushed herself to pursue her goals; she still exercised and still had a very bright vision of her future and that of her family.

Who do you think had more days in bed?

Can you see how the thinking leads to the feeling, which leads to the action (or in-action)?

Both women are now living what I would describe as full and healthy lives with some, "The Universe Says It's Time to Rest," days thrown in the mix. The woman in the first story just needed more sessions with me to undo and recreate her perceptions of the way she felt about herself and her life.

One of my favourite testimonials on my website is from a client whose husband said: "I don't know what you're doing, but keep doing it." When we make the most of life, we really do bring lightness not only to ourselves but to all of those around us too.

The internet, bookshops, inspirational groups and television shows have a seemingly limitless supply of inspirational stories. People, the world over, have survived and thrived after receiving death-sentence medical diagnoses, losing loved ones and experiencing other devastating life crises. What is the difference that makes the difference with those people? I think it's how much energy people expend focusing on what they can't do, be and have as opposed to how much energy they spend focusing on all the things they can do, be and have.

My mother was diagnosed with very serious macular degeneration in her early 40's. Her diagnosis was shocking and I'll never forget her tears as she told us that she was facing losing her license to drive and likely becoming blind within her 50's. So, what did she do? She booked lots of holidays to her dream destinations like Paris, Venice and Egypt so that she could experience those places while she still had her sight. She got the best advice she could get her hands, eyes and ears on about natural remedies. She followed that advice and cut many of her favourite foods out of her diet and added in what had been shown in research to improve her condition. She invested in high quality supplements and lifestyle changes where needed. Mum is now in her mid-60s and still driving and celebrating all that she can still do. Each day of sight is a blessing rather than another step towards some horrible, depressing doom. At her last check-up her eyes were exactly the same as her last visit—no further degeneration! I credit that to her physical, mental and energetic action to be positive and take 100% control of all the elements she can.

Making the most of your physical being, regardless of what you've considered to be your limitations will actually do wonders for your immune system and energy levels. Try it and see. If you do suffer from any health issues, I want you to try something for yourself: from now until the end of this book, unless you are in a medical appointment where symptoms must be discussed, do not talk about what's wrong—at all—ever! When someone asks how you are, say you're doing great. Look back on Day 25 and all those things that you're grateful to your body for and focus on them when you say, "I'm really good thanks!"

Having to check your insulin or give yourself daily injections can be interpreted as a heavy, depressing burden or just something you need to do each day like shaving or lacing up your shoes.

If you simply must research your disorder then look up what helps your condition, across all modalities and cultures. I have seen completely amazing turn-a-rounds in my work—clients living symptom-free with incurable conditions. Modalities such as naturopathy, homeopathy, chiropractic care and acupuncture can eliminate the need for surgery in many cases. This is not a bash on Western medicine. When I broke my femur, I wouldn't have wanted to be anywhere else but under the care of a highly trained western medical surgeon! There are however, fantastic centres the world over that support people who are having western medical treatments such as chemotherapy by teaching meditation and supplementing nutritionally. It's always worth getting a second opinion and looking at different modalities to have a wholistic approach and be helped in multiple ways.

Get to know your body. Look through this book for ideas on raising your vibration because that will help with every disease and illness that I've ever come across and give your immune system more energy to do what it needs to do. Choose to eat the most alive food you can. Research the positive things you can do for your health. Find a health professional that you feel good about and ask for some positive advice on increasing your options for feeling more healthy and vital. If they say there aren't any then vote with your feet and keep on looking because the world is filled with extremely talented professionals who are specialised in helping people in your exact situation. We now live in a global community so get on the internet and make it happen.

You are so powerful and you get to choose what you eat, what you think, what you say, what you focus on and how much time you invest into feeling great, whatever your circumstances.

Today's Commitment to Authentic Personal Power

Ask yourself:

What needs to happen for me to be at *cause* for my current health?

What step can I take today that will move me in the direction of loving appreciation for my miraculous body?

And now . . . take that step.

DAY 31

Social Interaction

*How to make the most of being a person
in the world who is surrounded by other people*

There's a reason we didn't all get our own planet (other than the obvious reproduction issues)—we need each other to learn and grow and be challenged to go deeper into new knowledge of ourselves. Our intense reactions, as goal posts for our next steps, usually happen in relating with the world outside us. In short—other people are really, really important!

Remember back to Day 5, during this day and the previous four; you learned just how other people highlight what you already have inside you. On Day 20, you learned how your personal frequency alters your perceptions. Without saying it overtly, all through this book you've been getting the message that other people are crucial features in the mastering of your authentic personal power.

Let me put it to you this way: I have some clients who have seen me for a session here and there for up to ten years. With these kinds of clients I get to see the growth and change that happens at, let's say "normal" rates (without the acceleration of more regular healing, coaching, and support). The people, in whom I see the least change, even over many years, are often those who have chosen to live the most solitary lives. If you isolate yourself, you can be stagnating because you're missing the opportunity to see your traits reflected back at you. If you live alone, there isn't as obvious a signal when your energy's low because you're not being cranky at your loved ones without valid reasons. Your mind also has the freedom to run wild in totally illogical ways, perhaps even proving your lack of self-worth, because there's no one there to tell you that your logic is flawed. The opposite is also true. In isolation you can imagine yourself into being a "Super Star" with absolutely no issues what-so-ever, because no one is ever close enough to you to highlight any unresolved emotions.

Relationships and our responses to relating to the people we care about call us forth to go deeper into ourselves. They also call us forth to be more open, to expand, to be known and loved.

In later days, we're going to talk about touch and sensuality, and often other people are involved there, too. You can hug yourself, but there's nothing quite like a hug or a snuggle-up with someone you adore who is radiating love and acceptance of all that you are.

There are many ways of getting to know yourself better and countless ways of getting to love "the you," that you uncover. Through communicating with other people, in meaningful relationships where you care about the impact you have, you can really see yourself with new eyes—the good, the bad and the ugly, and be supported to change what you wish to.

There are many definitions and uses of the words *introvert* and *extrovert*. In my work, I use *introvert* to describe people who process their emotions internally—so all by themselves in the privacy of their minds—and then express to whomever they need to afterwards with their understanding of what's happened, their feelings or whatever needs to be shared. I describe an *extrovert* as someone who processes emotions externally—out loud, normally with someone else—and who only arrives at understanding their feelings and responses, and what they want to do or say about them, in the process of communicating externally. Neither is better or worse or more or less evolved—we're all just different. For those of you who are extroverted, by my definition, you really need other people or you'll drown in internal dialogue and be getting nowhere fast.

When I was in my early 20s I travelled a lot. Other than my passion for other cultures, languages and new experiences it also gave me a break from realising just how much help I needed. I didn't know anyone well enough who would say to me, "Do you really think *that* is a wise idea?" Or "I'm worried about you," because no one had bonds strong enough to care. I could be a different person every day and the contradictions would never be noticed. But everywhere I moved to, I always took me with *me*, and eventually all that needed work would surface. Now, in my late 30s, loving my home base and fully reconnected to my family and some very close friends, I know myself and am able to love myself more than I ever dreamed possible. Every single transformation came from interacting with other people. Teachers, healers, friends, groups, workmates, people I loved, people I couldn't stand, people that disappointed me, people that pleasantly surprised me, people that role modelled ways of "being" that I disrespected or respected, people that I hurt and those that hurt me, people that broke my heart and the people that helped me mend it.

Our intimate relationships also teach us a great deal. I just couldn't be who I am today without all the relationships that have come before this moment in time. For many, many years my relationships highlighted my distinct lack of and ability to set boundaries and honour myself.

As I grew and changed, they taught me more and more about myself and all that I yearned to experience.

When you invest in relationships, they give back to you in amazing ways. Close friends can say, "I am watching you accept the unacceptable in that situation and I want for you to know that I think you deserve better," and then be there, loving you, regardless of what you choose to do. They can also say, "The way you are treating that person is painful to watch and it's not like you. What is going on?"

Other people give us new perspectives that can shake us up and have us question ourselves—which is one essential tool for personal growth. Other people's perspectives can also help us to solidify what we already believe. Sometimes in arguing for what you believe to be right and true, you connect with more certainty to your beliefs and values.

Before I became a parent, watching other parents helped me to hone in on what I really didn't want to ever do or create in my own children. It also solidified what I wanted to emulate and do similarly or the same. Watching how other people treat their partners, children, garden or even their hair can show us what we want to avoid or create for ourselves.

We need other people for the ideas of how to grow, change and improve.

Did your inspiration for reading this book come from seeing someone who appears to be genuinely empowered and happy? And to quote the line from, When Harry Met Sally, you've seen that and said to yourself: "I want what she's having?"

What have your relationships taught you?

All of them have had value, you know.

What do they continue to teach you?

I like the idea that people come into your life for a reason, a season, or a lifetime. I ask you to honour the relationships that you have (and have had) for all that they've highlighted for you. And I ask you to make the changes you feel are necessary to improve the ones that you're going to choose to keep.

Remembering that nothing is solid and everything is actually energy, think now about the energy exchange in your interactions with other people as well. When you're interacting with a happy, positive person, it lifts your energy (unless you are totally committed to being miserable, which is always a choice you have available). When you are interacting with someone who is negative about life and only says mean things about other people, it can lower your vibration (unless you are totally committed to seeing the positives in all people, places and experiences). The more happy, positive people there are, the higher the lift and the same is true in the opposite example. Think about the energy at a huge rock concert, surrounded by thousands of other fans, the lights are out, the headline act that everyone's paid their money to see is about the play the first note . . . it's electric, is it not? The energy is alive with excitement and expectation.

One of the best energetically uplifting experiences of my life was at the end of a U2 concert in Melbourne, Australia in 1989. Bono, the lead singer, had just talked about the charity they were supporting and letting us know that there would be people outside the venue for us to donate to if we wished to and then the band played '40'. It felt to me as though the whole crowd sang that song. I still get goose bumps every single time I think about it. As the concert finished, hundreds of us were still singing the final lines of the song, over and over as a huge group, strangers arm in arm, singing, and people were donating money to this worthy cause . . . there was no separation between any of us, all in sync . . . just magic! This is the power of energy exchange.

Today's Commitment to Authentic Personal Power

Who in your life has taught you the most about yourself?

If you previously considered this person to have been a harmful or hurtful influence in your life, can you allow this to change your perception of them?

What energy do you bring to your relationships and social situations?

Can you uplift people with your presence?

How and when do you do that?

How and when can you do more of that?

Day 32

Men & Women

Myth busting popular sexism

I cannot write about sexism without acknowledging some truth still present in our societies. There is sexism and limiting beliefs that we can all hold about our own gender and the opposite sex and this is what today is about. That said, male violence remains the leading cause of death, disability and illness for women in many countries across the world. In the overwhelming majority of cases, the men involved are known to the victims, often being their partners or family members. The percentages of these crimes being reported to authorities and the resulting percentage where a conviction takes place are alarmingly low and speak of broader social problems and tolerance of the unacceptable.

In my work I am focused on the individual human being and their personal relationships. On that level I see self-limiting sexism going both ways, and occurring in ways that don't serve either gender.

The clients I work with have a few things in common. Firstly, they want improvements in their life and are investing time and money into that outcome. Someone who makes this kind of commitment to themselves is generally aware of at least one of the following things: 1) Positive improvements are possible and 2) They deserve those improvements or will make that worthiness part of the improvement process. From the first session onwards they are aware of being at *cause* and *effect* and if they continue with this work, responsibility is taken for owning the lead role in their life creation. Not everyone is ready for nor interested in this kind of self empowerment and for this reason I am under no delusion that I am working with a good cross section of society. People who think they have no issues don't generally seek help. Likewise, people who expect to be and think they deserve to be treated appallingly often don't look for help to fix things either.

Today is written outside of the context of the larger world issues relating to gender. It is specifically looking at you, as an individual, and what you believe about men and women.

245

While there are horrifying statistics relating to gender, they are no different to any other kind of generalisation. There are peaceful, kind men and violent, cruel women and vice versa. It is time to judge individuals based on the individual themselves, not the colour of their skin, their gender, their sexual preference, hair colour or any other issue that has nothing to do with the essence of them as a being. Whilst most children are probably raised with certain biases based on their gender, each individual has the same inherent capacity for growth and change.

What could be possible if all of your sexist, pre-conceived ideas about the traits of men and women just disappeared? I wholeheartedly believe there are no fundamental truths about the stereotypes of men and women.

I grew up in a society after the feminist revolution where I expected to be able to vote and be paid an equal amount for doing the same job as a man. I found the idea of men and women not being treated equally ridiculous to contemplate because it just purely didn't make sense that it could be any other way. Unfortunately, as I grew up I observed some men who belittled women down as overly emotional, wingy naggers and also observed women who put men down by claiming they were less in touch with their emotions, less able to communicate, less able to find things and not willing to ask for directions. I do understand that men and women feel superior to each other for various reasons, not the least of which is centuries of female of oppression. It's time however for all the stereotyping to stop!

When I started having relationships with men as an adult, I commited to men who had values, opinions, behaviours, and actions which I did not respect. I desperately wanted these men to love and approve of me (so much so that I would go against my beliefs and standards just to please them). I actually just didn't know how to respect myself or the men in my relationships. Sadly, this is not uncommon. So many of the women I've worked with have divided men into two categories: ones they are frightened or intimidated by and those they feel superior to. There is often very little middle ground.

The belittling of men is really prominent in Australian advertising too, and this is to appeal to the female market. I see these advertisements and cringe. The between-the-lines messages are things like: this washing machine is so easy to use that even your utterly hopeless husband can still put a load on. I was at a friend's birthday recently and there was a group of children playing with soft-projectile gun things. There was a seven-year-old girl who had a couple of shots and said, "Not bad for a girl," a few times. The female adults took turns in telling her that girls were actually better than boys at everything. Throughout this book, you've learned all the ways in which you are creating your reality, with your mind, body and vibration. It really is time for us as a global community to stop with the verbal women-bashing and men-bashing that is occurring when we are in groups of our own gender.

Read these and see what pops into your head:

Men are just after one thing . . .

Women are just after one thing . . .

Men are always doing that . . .

Women are always doing that . . .

What are your preconceived notions? How many others do you think you have?

As a therapist, I've have the honour of being invited into the private, inner world of hundreds of people and it has allowed me to completely dissolve any preconceived notions of how women and men are. Now I see that every single relationship is a co-created dance.

Many people come to me for help, ready to end long-term relationships because they cannot stand the other person's behaviour. We work through the same model you've been presented with in this book, and the client steps into *cause* to understand all the meanings they've been making. After they engage in the exercises you've been learning many of the relationships end up surviving. There is often a process of the client owning their own sub-standard behaviour and a deep understanding of how they have co-created the disharmony they blamed the other person for.

Throughout the years I have worked with an ever-increasing number of men. As I started to see stay-at-home dads who were partnered with full-time working women, I learned even more. The hurt, complaints, frustrations, rejections, and dissatisfactions of the stay-at-home dads were often exactly the same as for the stay-at-home mums I'd seen. The issues for the income-producing partner were often the same, too, regardless of gender.

I've worked with countless women facing rejection, hurt, and anger caused by the lack of physical intimacy and sex with their male partners. I've worked with men who are looking for tools to try and get their female partners to talk about their feelings more, because the man has no idea what's going on with her.

For every time a woman tells me a story of woe and finishes it by saying, "That's just how men are," I am in the position of having heard a man share a very similar story where the offender is female. I have found the same issues exist in same-sex relationships too. So, guess what? We're all just actually people. Human beings are wonderfully varied. However, the equipment in your underpants honestly has very little to do with this variation—believe me!

Okay, I'm climbing off my soap box now. I just want to tell you (in case you haven't already guessed) WHY this is good to know. If you think all men are emotionally underdeveloped; guess what—you'll attract lots of experiences in your life to prove yourself correct. Your mind is attracted to things that make sense, so you will just 'click' with men that make sense to you (and they'll have issues with emotional maturity because that's what you're expecting them to be like). If you think all women are lying cheaters after the man with the biggest bank balance; guess what—you'll be meeting lots of these women because that's what you're expecting. If you think men do as little as they can get away with domestically, then guess what—you're going to get just that (and not be surprised about it at all!) If you think women always complain and whatever you do is just not good enough; then guess what—right again!

Remember, change 'you' and it changes the world around you.

Time after time I work with clients who hold to rigid certainties about their own gender and the opposite sex. Time after time, as we release these beliefs, the clients are able to go out into their futures and transform their relationships and I hear, "I never knew there were men/women like this."

You get what you expect and yet, even in many 'spiritual' communities, there is still talk about the opposite sex as if they have a defect. If you want to have mutually respectful relationships, to value and respect the opposite sex, and feel valued and respected by them, then it's time to release your sexist limitations.

I was at a three-day festival once and on Day 1, I met a man in line waiting for food. He was telling me about 'women' and that we were 'all alike'. He was in his thirties and never had a relationship with a woman who wanted anything more meaningful than physical sex. He felt used and honestly held the view that all women were just after that one thing because in his experience, he was right. He loved sex, but he yearned for an emotional, meaningful, and long-term connection. He had given up on finding it. We talked through the line and ended up having lunch together. On Day 3, he ran up to me and shared that since our conversation, he'd met heaps of amazing women at the festival. He thanked me for opening up his mind.

The other fascinating behaviours I see as a therapist are the extremely common double standards and sexist hypocrisy. When a man does something, it is interpreted in one way and when a woman does exactly the same thing it is interpreted completely differently (and the same in reverse). Let me give an example from my experience: I worked with a couple once that were mutually dissatisfied. When the man would set boundaries with his wife for how he would agree to be treated and communicate ideas for the way forward he considered this to be assertive (a natural by-product of his confidence). When his partner would set boundaries with him for how she would agree to be treated and communicate her ideas for the way forward he considered this to be bossy and needy (a natural by-product of her manipulative nature and low self esteem). In actual fact, they were both confident and wanting to work on the relationship.

What are your double standards? What do you think is OK for one sex but inappropriate for the other? Do you want to keep those limitations? What positive purpose do they serve?

What I hope you've gained from reading through today is an ability to question yourself in and around this topic. If you can use all the tools that have come before, and step into cause in this very important area of your life, you will be able to appreciate the beauty of the differences between men and women without attaching negative and harmful meanings.

Today's Commitment to Authentic Personal Power

First, I want you to delve deep into what you believe about men and women. And what counter examples you have already from your own experience or other people you've heard or read about. My story above, about the man at the festival, is an example of what I mean.

What I believe men are like:

Counter example:

What I believe women are like:

Counter example:

Now, ask yourself: what would be possible if I assessed the character of every single person I met based on them as a human being, without taking into account their gender?

Lastly, for the next 24 hours commit to not entering any conversation that puts anyone down based on their gender and be alert to any of your or other people's biases, too.

DAY 33

The Importance of a Sensual Life—Part 1

Wholistic delighting of your senses

Our magical, human bodies are sensual inside and all over. *Sensual* in this instance is referring to all of our senses, the big five: sight, hearing, smelling, tasting, feeling and the less commonly acknowledged ability to sense energy. I'm not referring to, "I see dead people," like in *The Sixth Sense*, but instead to our ability to sense our environment in a way that is beyond the other five senses. When you walk into a room where there's been a fight, it's a different thing to walking into a room where people have just made love. When you walk into a clean and fresh smelling, empty bar where people have been drinking for years, it feels very different to when you walk into a clean and fresh smelling, empty church. This sense of difference goes beyond what you can see and smell. All human beings have this ability.

How often do you delight your senses?

What do you look at that is a pleasure to see?

What do you listen to that is a pleasure to hear?

What pleasurable fragrances do you regularly experience?

What do you eat that feels fantastic in your mouth and tastes delicious?

Your physical being is covered with feeling receptors—what do you do to send data down these receptors so you are able to experience pleasurable sensations?

What high-vibrational people and places are you familiar with?

251

Whilst I am taking the time to separate out these senses for the purpose of explanation, all the senses work together to create a sensually pleasurable life. Eating a meal that looks, tastes, and smells delicious in a restaurant overlooking the sea with a great atmosphere and company is much more pleasurable than eating the same meal on your own in a cold room looking at a blank wall. The reason is because our senses work together in the creation of rich life experiences.

It is always a good thing to go out of your way to have new sensual experiences—it broadens the brain and opens new possibilities for pleasure. Healthy pleasure lifts and expands your vibration, too. So, get out there and try new food and drinks. Listen to new music. Seek new fabrics, colours, and art. Go to different climates and see nature in as many forms as possible. If you've only ever swam in salt water, get into some fresh water. If you've only ever swam in warm tropical water, go run into a cold ocean to experience the sensations that rush into your being. If you've done lots of scuba diving or snorkelling, but you've never appreciated the world from above, go hang gliding or get in a helicopter. If stuff like that is out of your current financial reach, then get your hands on a book of aerial photos and imagine yourself up there seeing those sights and breathing in the fresh air. If you like electronic, dance music then listen to some classical music up loud on a great stereo or some chanting or ambient forest sounds. When was the last time you smelled an organic, pure essential oil of any kind?

How often can you delight your senses more often?

What new visual experiences can you seek out and experience more of?

What range of sounds do you have access to right now?

What pleasurable fragrances do you have in your surroundings and what extra ones can you seek out to experience?

What new and interesting, tasty and healthy foods and drinks would you like to try? And where can you find out about even more?

How often are you touched? How often do you take the time to stop, hug and be hugged by the meaningful people in your life? If it feels good to you, do it more often.

Do you really want a sensational life? And if so, what are you going to do about it?

What new actions can you take for daily sensual pleasure?

Have you ever heard it said that babies need to be touched in order to grow properly? According to Bridget Coila, "Lack of physical contact can prevent normal development and can even lead to higher rates of illness or death in infants." *http://www.livestrong.com/article/72120-effect-human-contact-newborn-babies/*. I have a friend who teaches baby massage to new parents and was amazed by what I learned through her as she was training. There is so much evidence supporting the power of human touch, especially with babies born prematurely.

Love and touch actually causes children's brains to grow, according to Marian Diamond, a neuroscientist at the University of California, Berkeley, and author of *Magic Trees of the Mind: How to Nurture Your Child's Intelligence, Creativity, and Healthy Emotions From Birth Through Adolescence.*

I hear this stuff and think—we're all still human beings. Just because we grew up and learned to do things for ourselves, the basic requirements of love and touch didn't go away.

How often do you connect with yourself through touch?

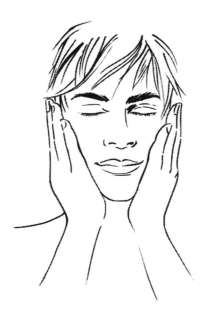

Before the end of today, take the time to cup the jaw and cheek of one of the sides of your face with your own hand. Rest there for a moment, breathe slowly and deeply into the experience and see how it feels to really connect with 'You' in this way. Close your eyes . . . how does that feel for your face? How does it feel for your hand? If it feels nice then do the same for the other side of your face. Try sliding one of your hands up into your hair line . . . how does that feel?

So many people (single and in relationships), crave physical intimacy without knowing the simple, intimate connections they can have with themselves. One of the most important tools in *Ayurvedic* medicine, practiced in India for over 5,000 years, is *Abhyanga*—self massage. This practice of massaging your skin with warmed oil releases a whole host of healing compounds with positive effects for every level of your being. It feels good, detoxifies, improves circulation, boosts immune function, calms the mind and slows the aging process. Put simply—touch is very, very good for you!

How comfortable are you with prioritising things that feel good for your body? Does it feel selfish and indulgent? Does it already make total sense? Is it easy for you to take the time to please your senses by going to beautiful places, smelling and tasting yummy things and hearing enjoyable sounds? How easy would it be to create more enjoyable experiences for your senses in daily life?

Today's Commitment to Authentic Personal Power

Choose one of your senses to delight and focus on for the day, giving yourself the rich experience of prioritising that part of your sensual life.

Take the time to notice how you feel physically, mentally and energetically before, during, and after each experience.

Day 34

The Importance of a
Sensual Life—Part 2

Let's talk about sex

"Let's talk about sex, baby. Let's talk about you and me.
Let's talk about all the good things, and the bad things, that may be"
Salt 'n' Pepa

I think Salt 'n' Pepa had it right when they rapped out their "Let's Talk about Sex" track back in 1990. They were discussing practicing safe sex and the side effects of censorship in mainstream media. The song also talked about a woman whose "body was booming," but rather than being glad about all the male attention and sexual relationships she attracted she was "mad, and sad and feeling bad." This was because she didn't feel loved in those interactions and, reading between the lines, wasn't able to ask for what she wanted. Can you identify with either of these ideas? It is not uncommon for couples to avoid talking about avoiding pregnancy and likewise conversations about fertility and trying to create pregnancy. Lack of genuine communication is also very common in many sexual relationships. Things as simple as likes, dislikes and new ideas are often suppressed by one or both of the partners. I couldn't count the number of times a client has replied with "I couldn't say *that*!" when I've suggested a more direct expression about the state of their sexual relationship.

How would you rate the honesty, openness, and quality of your conversations about sex with partners in the past and your 'now'?

I think we should all be talking about sex more—with our partners and honestly and openly with ourselves. I find it totally bizarre how many personal development books exist that don't talk about sex. It's the elephant in the room when it comes to our self-image and esteem. Sensual, sexual experiences between consenting adults are fantastically healthy for you on every level of your being. It builds self-belief, it's great exercise, and it lifts your vibration. Like a dance, you and your partner must be aware of the other, giving and receiving, so it's a shared experience mentally, physically and energetically. Great sex requires some confidence and ability to be open and vulnerable at the same time. Your sex life really can be a personal development journey in and of itself with powerful flow-on results physically, mentally, emotionally and energetically. Those effects can be powerfully good or bad—depending on your communication and care.

Let me give you an analogy: traffic can flow together in harmony if people are courteous to one another, mindful of their surroundings, and communicate properly (indicators, brake lights, etc.). We've all experienced madness on the road. It's chaotic right? And all of these factors can lead to a big, harmful crash. Likewise, sexual relationships with bad communication and lack of care can result in emotional implosions or explosions. These results can both be avoided with honest communication. When a couple is driving together in a car, the driving can be hold-onto-your-hats fast (so fast it's like a Grand Prix race) or it can be slow and scenic. Both work beautifully well when the couple wants the same thing. If one person is in a huge hurry and the other one wants to stop every few minutes and photograph the scenery this is where problems start—with lack of communication and compromise. Whether the passenger is shouting out to slow the hell down or the driver is taking the time to notice that the passenger isn't having such a good time is neither here nor there. Both people can be at *cause* for the outcomes they are creating—so no blame, just communication required. A good and safe, mutually enjoyable drive requires communication and care. Similarly, if you're going to car pool with a total stranger it might be a good idea to check in with what kind of driving style they prefer, before you get in the car.

Feeling comfortable to talk with your partner about the sex you're having or want to be having will result in more enjoyable sex for both of you. In loving relationships, it will also build a closer emotional bond.

You can learn a LOT about yourself by having a good look at how you think and feel about yourself sexually. Whether you're partnered or not, for most of your life having sex drive is a healthy sign of vitality and being connected with your authentic personal power. I'm not saying you have to be out on dance floors flaunting your stuff; I am saying that sexual energy is a wonderful part of a healthy life. It is also one of the many gifts of being a human being.

What comes to mind when you hear the words sex or making love? Do you get embarrassed or think: "Yay, yes please" or somewhere in-between?

It is astounding to me, as a therapist, what many people will say is "fine" in their partnerships sexually. However, with the smallest amount of questioning it soon becomes apparent, things aren't fine but actually emotionally very painful and not being talked about. If you are in a sexual relationship, how often do you communicate about the sex you're having or, as the case may be, *not* having?

"Give me a little of that human touch," Bruce Springsteen.

As luck would have it, sitting here completing the final edit before this book heads off to be published, a Bruce Springsteen song is on. He just toured Australia and I had the chance to see him perform the song, "Human Touch." He sings of a woman prizing emotional safety over human connection and says: "You can't shut off the risk and the pain without losing the love that remains." I have seen, very recently, at his concert, how much that song resonated with hundreds of people. During my years as a therapist, I have seen this pattern again and again with men and women alike. If you have made a decision, from a place of pain, to shut down to your sensual and sexual drive please take some time to review that decision. This doesn't mean you need to rush out on to the relationship scene straight away (or ever if that's what you choose) but if you are shut off in that area, why not take the time to create a relationship with yourself, even if it's just for your health.

Did you know that orgasms are extremely good for you? Lack of orgasms in your life creates energetic stagnation. Having orgasms regularly in your life energetically cleanses and raises your vibration. That said, there is also a lot of research that's been done on the health benefits of orgasms also. Cosmopolitan even did a feature on the top ten benefits of orgasms, *http://www.cosmopolitan.com/sex-love/advice/orgasm-health-benefits#*. Here are some excerpts from the list:

- **The Best Medicine**: A visit from Dr. Feelgood, a.k.a. an orgasm, releases endorphins that produce euphoria, pleasure, and occasionally uncontrollable laughter.
- **The Actual Cure for the Common Cold**: Forget apples. Fornicating regularly keeps the doctor away. Sexual health counselor and researcher Alison Richardson says: "Regular sex is linked to higher levels of the antibody immunoglobulin A, which may protect us from common colds by boosting the immune system."
- **After Sex the Glass is Half Full**: It's good for your head as well as your heart and, uh, those other very special parts too! Sexual hormones may lower rates of depression, anxiety and suicide. Doing the horizontal mambo relieves everyday tension as well . . .

- **Battling Breast Cancer the Fun Way**: According to Needle, Oxytocin has been shown to possibly prevent breast cancer cells from developing into a tumor. And don't forget the foreplay! Breast and nipple stimulation produces even more cancer-cell-fighting oxytocin.

The Queen's University in Belfast, Ireland did a study in 2001 into the health benefits of sex to culmination no less than three times a week. The results suggested that it reduced the risk of heart attack or stroke in males by half.

If you want to read more about this topic then I suggest you read a book by Eric R. Braverman, MD titled, *Younger Sexier You*. The cover says it all: "Enjoy the Best Sex of Your Life and Look and Feel Years Younger. This is a book to put you back together and restore your brain health, leading to great, mature, free and easy grown-up sex . . . the best kind."

Today's Commitment to Authentic Personal Power

Talk about what you've learned today with someone. If you already knew it all, then keep on sharing the news that sex and orgasms are fantastic for ongoing, wholistic health.

If you had a light bulb moment while reading today, then I want you to begin working on that area. Just begin—you don't have to instantly transform out of your comfort zone, but how would it feel if you were just able to begin?

This beginning may take the form of getting some support from a therapist, or having a conversation with your partner. It may involve some self-exploration, mentally or physically. Only you know where you need to begin and if you're not sure then head back up to the first part of today's commitment which is: Talk about what you've learned with someone. Ideally that person would be someone with a very positive attitude towards the topic.

Day 35

How Your Mind can Positively Uplift Your Body and Energy Levels

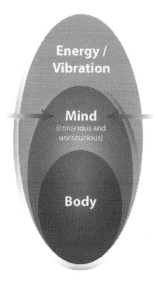

There are three main points to keep in mind about your mind in this context:

1. Your mind is like a very-efficient and super-speedy librarian. When you consciously request information about snails, your mind, like a speedy librarian, can bring up all the references in your memory. Depending on your experiences you may remember books you have read or the incident where you had a snail invasion in your vegie garden. When you consciously think, "No one likes me," your 'librarian' goes to work with all the experiences available 'on file'. People with close friends, a partner that loves them, and who are active in their community can even fall victim to believing the, "No one likes me," thought. This is how respectful your librarian is—it will give you whatever you ask for, no matter how obscure it is. It will delve in and find you some sort of evidence to back-up your thought. It doesn't mean that everything it finds is realistic or true, for example, no matter how much some of us wish it to be, there aren't

human-sized, devastatingly beautiful elves living in the forests. Your unconscious mind holds the records of every perception that's come in through your senses. When you upload all that old data as 'evidence' for your current thinking you live and breathe it as if it were the truth. You'll always have your *proover department* but don't believe everything you think.

Take a moment now to imagine walking into an organic grocery store and see, in your minds' eye, the fruit and vegetable section. All the fruit and vegetables look colourful and inviting. There are samples of everything on white plates in front of all the fruit. You see your favourite fruit, cut up in your favourite way and knowing the store wants you to taste the difference of organic produce, you take a piece and pop it in your mouth . . . delicious . . . possibly the best experience of this fruit in your whole life. Now walk up to the lemons for sale, see the samples, pick up a section of lemon and sink your teeth into it, getting a mouth full of that juice . . .

What happened in your mouth?

Your mind can produce many responses to the things you are imagining. So remember back to Day 23 and use your imagination for the power of positivity. You will then have your librarian finding all the references for all the positive stuff you've got in your library of life records.

2. Each thought has a frequency that interacts with and affects your body and energy levels. This frequency determines whether you feel heavy, *blurky*, like everything is hard, and stays attached to the lower-frequency parts of your unconscious program. On the contrary, you can feel light and free, like everything's easy, and access the positivity.

Those thoughts create emotions the body experiences and they also affect you energetically. I don't think there would be any health modalities that suggest that prolonged emotional stress is anything other than damaging to your physical and mental health. This demonstrates the power of your mind over body.

Thinking sinks into your entire body. It affects your posture, and breathing which adds to the spiral upwards or downwards. Thinking also radiates out and through your energy, uplifting or polluting your vibration. Just like in a watch, each cog makes the others turn. Within you, your thinking can set off a positive and uplifting chain reaction or negative downward spiral.

It takes one differently-charged thought to change the direction of your cogs and get your spiral moving in an upwards direction.

During the first 17 days of this book, we worked through a lot of your mental programming and old ways of thinking. As you experienced positive shifts into a more empowering perspective, how did that change affect your energy? What happened in your body as a result? Things like posture and breath will change as you like and accept yourself more often.

3. Your thoughts and feelings about any actions you're thinking of taking will directly affect the effort you put into those actions. The level of effort you put into your actions will directly affect the results you get. In the words of Henry Ford, "Whether you think you can or think you can't, you're right."

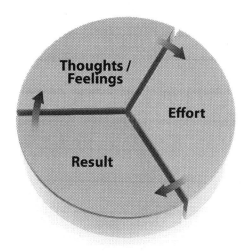

I see many clients who are living self-fulfilling prophesies based on what they already thought would happen. There have been many examples of this in action already in this book. Let me give you another one: Aaron came to me as a tired and frustrated single parent, widowed the previous year. Following his wife's death the care of their children, then four and eight, became entirely Aaron's responsibility. His parents lived overseas and there was no other extended family to support him regularly. He grew up doing chores around the house and wanted to instil the same values in his children. He gave them basic tasks to complete on a daily basis. If I put a number on it, I would say he was 20% sure that his children would follow through with completing their allotted tasks. So, keeping in mind Aaron's emotional circumstances, can you imagine how he felt being the sole income earning, responsible adult in the house? How much energy do you think he was investing in making sure his children finished their chores before they went to day care and school, and he to work? I'd say he was putting in 20% effort, sometimes a lot more and sometimes a lot less depending on his energy levels, but we're talking about averages here. Based on his current circumstances, what do you think his results were like? Does it make sense that his ratio of tasks done vs. tasks left undone was 20-80?

Looking at the diagram above, can you think of an example in your own life where the % of effort you put in matches the quality of results you got?

This is a very useful framework to remember. How you think will generate how you feel. How you feel will be the major contributor in your quality of action i.e. how much effort you put in. That energy of effort, combined with whether you believe in your ability will impact the result.

This is also true when putting energy into new relationships, finding new work, keeping your garden looking neat, connecting with your power and all other activities you engage in.

Many remarkable discoveries and inventions have come into being by accident, just like there are countless stories of successful men and women that fail on their way to the top. Having the mindset that you *will* get there creates the energy to put 100% effort into your action. This continuing effort, combined with the process of trial and correction will pay off in results.

> *"Try not;*
> *do*
> *or do not,*
> *there is no try"*
> Yoda

Sometimes, when you're truly stuck in icky thinking it is best to get your body moving or change your energy levels as step one rather than trying to fight thoughts with thoughts. This is the reason why it's essential to understand your innate resources of mind, body and energy as the system that they are. You always have the choice to feel better by starting with one of these three areas. In any given moment, there will be one that shifts the easiest—so start there.

Today's Commitment to Authentic Personal Power

Choose an affirmation for the day. You can go back to the one you created on Day 13 or use the instructions to craft a new one with the same principles. As often as you remember throughout the day, repeat this affirmation repetitively (like a broken record). When you have some spare brain-space, take the time to imagine (for the purpose of positivity) bringing your affirmation to life and seeing it come into fruition. In your mind's eye, imagine you're already living and breathing the truth of its presence, seeing, hearing, and feeling what it will be like when it becomes your 'now'.

Notice the positive effects of your affirmation emotionally, physically and energetically.

Enjoy!

How Your Body can Positively Uplift Your Mind and Vibration

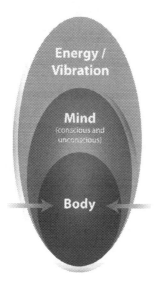

None of your thoughts, feelings, actions and experiences are possible without your body. Your belief system along with the creation and experience of your reality, are not possible without a body either.

For me, living in and being an inseparable part of a vibrational universe becomes all the more exciting when I appreciate that energy is flowing through my physical vehicle—I am not a solid object. Not only that but it's actually energy that keeps my physical body together rather than having the little bits of matter fly off in random directions. It's the same energy that our planet is mostly made up of, the same energy that keeps our Earth predictably travelling around our Sun and it's the same energy that this book you're reading is mostly made of (whether it's paper or some kind of electronic reader). So this energy is all around us, and running through us and what I do with my physical body can enhance or decrease how much freedom, flow, power, and control I feel in my daily experiences.

Being more physically flexible allows more life-force to flow through your being—this is one of the many benefits of practicing yogic postures. Exercise of any kind raises your energy (unless you choose to run two marathons in a row . . . that would lower your energy . . . so perhaps don't do that!). Higher vibration and more flow means that you are able to adjust your internal radio dial to tune in to higher quality thoughts. Let me borrow an analogy from my garden hose. When a garden hose is lying around for years it gets clogged with gunk. When you finally turn on the tap, some water will come out, but the flow will be slow and interrupted with chunks of dirt and glug from the inside. By massaging oil into the hose, section by section, and creating movement by bending and twisting the piping, we would dislodge the gunk inside. Once the gunk was cleared out we'd have, clean and fresh water running through at full capacity. Your body is exactly the same. It needs to bend and stretch, move, and be used or we become energetically clogged. This stagnation results in lower vibration and makes it easier to tap into the lower vibrations of your thought unconscious program. It also attracts you to low vibration foods, mindless television, and other inactivity. The great thing is that the same is exactly true in reverse. Energetic vitality brought about by eating high-quality food and exercising will lift your vibration, making it easier to tap into higher-vibration thoughts and creates a desire to match that energy with more high-vibration food choices and physical activities.

Physical activity gets things moving—all things—on all levels of your being.

Have you ever been stuck in a yucky emotional place and managed to get yourself out for a walk, to yoga or any other activity you can think of that gets you moving? It uplifts your mood, doesn't it? That physical movement is allowing you to access the uplifted parts of your mental program and all emotional states are magnetic. Anger attracts in more anger and joy attracts in more joy. Activity creates more activity. Stagnation and positive action cannot exist in the same 'now' any more than oil and water can stay together without separating out into their different densities.

Forcing your body up and out to move, whether you feel like it or not, is a spectacular way to quickly exit *blurk*ville. If you're 'stuck' at work, in the car, or in a time and place where moving too much just isn't an option then focus on your posture and breath. You've read the two days about breathing and the incredible impact that conscious breathing has on your physiology and energy levels. Consciously choosing your posture is also an immediate way to positively uplift the resources you can access physically, mentally and energetically.

When I am teaching conscious posture in my workshops I get participants to spend a couple of minutes in each of the stances above, hunched and slouched and then upright with arms open. If you are sufficiently slouched it is virtually impossible to use your lungs to anything near capacity. If you are standing up, with arms open it usually feels a bit silly to breathe in a short and shallow way, so breathing tends to deepen and lengthen while in that stance. The lack of deep breath and general 'feeling' of being slouched makes it super easy to access lower vibrating thoughts and feelings. The intake of oxygen and general 'feeling' of being up and open to the world makes it much easier to access higher vibrating states like positivity, motivation, and inspiration. Every time I teach this tool I am reminded of the Charley Brown cartoon where he is explaining to Lucy about his 'depressed stance'. He informs her, "When you're depressed, it makes a lot of difference how you stand. The worst thing you can do is straighten up and hold your head high because then you'll start to feel better."

Just like I did in Day 19, I am referring here to people who are experiencing a depression that is an energetic heaviness and darkness coupled with low vibration thoughts and feelings (and I am not suggesting that all cases of depression are this way). In the cases I'm talking about, working with the client's innate resources has produced a complete turn-a-round to better, lighter and more empowered states of being. Working with the body using posture, breathing techniques, dietary improvements and exercise we begin the shift on that physical level. Regardless of the type of depression anybody is experiencing, the tools in this book, including conscious posture and breathing will support the body's ability to feel better and constrictive posture and short, shallow breath will support the body's ability to feel worse. My point is that, regardless of the medical diagnosis, there are things that every single person can do to improve their perspective of themselves and their lives.

Today's Commitment to Authentic Personal Power

Make a list of 10 physical activities that you know make you feel better. If you can't think of 10 then write as many as you can think of and add to the list as you spend more of the rest of your life at *cause*, trying new things and living authentically in your personal power. Believe me; the list will grow in the coming years.

Keep this list to refer back to and next time if you're in a *blurk* choose to do one of them!

1)

2)

3)

4)

5)

6)

7)

8)

9)

10)

How Your Energy can Positively Uplift Your Mind and Body

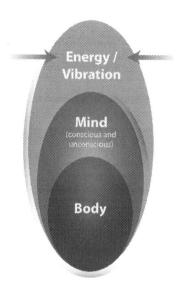

It has been very exciting for me to watch the changes in society's perception of 'energy' and 'energetic healing' since seeing my first client for Reiki healing in 1998. Reverend Beth Gray had brought Reiki to Australia in 1983 but even fifteen years onwards very few people I came across had heard of the modality or experienced its subtle, transformative power to support the body's innate healing ability to create health and vitality.

When I first began learning and practicing Reiki it was challenging for me to explain to new people what it was and how it worked. I was often met with scorn or disbelief that life-force energy even existed other than in science fiction and for most people it was quite 'wacky, woo-woo'. I laugh now when I think about those first explanations. I used to start by asking: "You know how you can sometimes 'feel' when someone is standing behind you, even if you can't see them and haven't heard them approach? Well that's because we all have an energy field." It was a convoluted way to try and find an energetic experience that the new person could identify with and then build my explanation from there. It often took a while before I even got around to explaining what energetic healing was, how it worked, and what it can do. Now, even the least alternative people I know are using therapies like acupuncture, a modality based on the principle that there are energetic pathways throughout the body that influence internal organs and structures. It is also very common to hear people from all walks of life talk about the "vibes" they got from a person or place. Awareness of energy has become much more commonplace and from my perspective, this is a fabulous thing.

Meditation has also been embraced in the West and it's hard to find someone who doesn't know what it is. Many people who know what it is have either tried it or think it may be a good thing for them to learn. There have been so many studies into the positive benefits of meditation for mind and body that there are even large corporate organisations that approve classes in their offices to support their staff in reducing stress and therefore increasing productivity. Keeping in mind that our physical bodies are predominantly vibrating energy, meditation is one of the fastest ways to lift your vibration and improve overall health.

Having low vibration is like trying to exist on planet Earth with double the current gravity. Everything is heavier, slower, and harder. By working directly with the energy that is within and all around your being, wonderful uplifting moments can occur in your thinking (and therefore feelings) and your physical health.

You now have the ability to choose to transform yourself and your experiences by embracing a higher vision and higher understanding of yourself. You already have the tools for this experience. You know now that you are an energetic being, having a human experience. You know now that the parts of you that are actually 'physical' would be invisible to the human eye if it weren't for your true, energetic nature. By taking the time and energy to regularly acknowledge this truth, you will forever transform your perception of yourself and your life, what's possible in your now and the future you're creating.

Profound changes have and are occurring for you as you read this book. Never, ever again do you need to have a mundane, dreary view about anything. You are vibrantly alive and by acknowledging this and tending to that aliveness you can grow in ways you may not have even thought of yet. No one can water, weed and nurture their garden if they don't know they have one. Likewise, now that you know about all the aliveness that's in your being you can choose to nourish and support its growth.

When your energy is free and clear, you will have mental clarity about yourself and your circumstances also. This means leaving behind fears, blame, negative imaginings and instead having easier access to inspiration, empowerment, and trusting your own wisdom. Free flowing, high and clear energy also creates a lightness of 'being' that supports physical health and vitality. It doesn't even matter if a person believes or doesn't believe in all this energy stuff, the tools you've learned in this book will still create powerful improvements.

I had a couple come to my qi going beginner's class many years ago. The husband thought it was all a load of hogwash and only came because his wife pleaded for his company. Initially, his mind was not convinced that there was any point being there, moving his body around and breathing in a different way than he was used to. His thoughts were particularly negative about their daily, five-minute practice on non-class days. As my classes begin each week, students have the opportunity to share experiences and ask questions. In week four of the eight week course, this man shared with surprise that he'd noticed during the week that the pain he'd had in his lower back for many, many years was no longer there. He had not changed any other aspect in his life and was able to attribute this massive life change to these classes and his short, daily practice of qi gong. The point of the story is this: even if you're stuck in negative thinking, doing something physical or energetic can create the shift. So, please, don't get stuck in fighting thoughts with thoughts, like the angel and the devil inside your mind fighting over whether something is the 'right' or 'wrong' thing—choose one of your other innate resources first and make the changes flow more easily.

Today's Commitment to Authentic Personal Power

Choose an activity that you know will uplift your energy.

It can be one of the items talked about on Day 24—Lifting Your Vibration Part 2, one of the many others discussed in this book or something that you just know, from your own experience results in you feeling lighter of body, heart and mind.

Take note of what you experience mentally, physically and energetically during each phase of:

1) Making the choice to do the chosen activity.
2) During the chosen activity.
3) And following the activity for the rest of your day.

DAY 38

Analysis Paralysis

Why it's time to stop asking "Why?"

"The secret of change is to focus all of your energy not into fighting the old but on building the new"—Socrates

I didn't coin the phrase 'analysis paralysis,' but I love it and use it often. There comes a time when we must stop discussing the same issues in the same way and make a decision to become part of a solution. Being at *cause* for your 'now' and your future is a strong and powerful place to reside. It's OK to drop out of there as often as you like, and feel sorry for yourself and upset when setbacks occur but really . . . how long do you want to stay there for?

How often have you, in the past, succumbed to an attack of the "whys"?

Why did I eat that second muffin?
Why don't they care about me?
Why have I woken up with a headache?
Why don't I have orgasms like other people seem to?
Why do some people get all the luck?
Why did I have to get sick?
Why? Why? Why?

Knowing all that you now know about being at *cause*, what skills do you already have to pop back out of an attack of the 'whys' if they surface again?

How to move from the why place to the wise place

The why place is very different to the wise place. Below are some instructions for how to get out of the why place. Once you're out of there, looking back on all you've learned as a result of that situation you were asking 'why' about—that's the wise place.

Here's an idea:

Why not answer the why question? Take whatever pops into your head as the answer and then ask:

How can I do it differently in the future? Or how can I make changes right now that will change things?

Or, in the more serious situations: What kind of support might be good to seek out so that I have some tools to cope in this situation?

To illustrate my point, I'll use the muffin example. Why, why, why did I eat that second muffin? The answer that pops into your head might be something like these:

a) Because I was hungry.
b) Because I'm lonely.
c) Because I deserve it.

Now, if you've sunk into the whys then I'm making that mean that you're not happy about the eating of the second muffin, so now it's time to ask the second part about what to change to not repeat the event.

a) How can I do it differently in the future? Well, on my next day off I could bake some really healthy treats or buy some healthy snacks so that next time I'm hungry I make a choice that I end up feeling really happy with. Done.

b) How can I make changes right now that will change things? Ok, I'm feeling lonely . . . the muffin is now gone and to be honest it wasn't that stimulating a conversationalist anyway so . . . who can I call, visit or connect with right now or when I'm next free? Make a plan to do so. If you are lonely because you don't currently have heart-felt relationships in your life then it's time to ask the same question, but for the purpose of thinking about ways to make new connections with like-minded people. Done.

c) OK, you deserve it but are now in the whys so it's time for: How can I do it differently in the future? What else do you deserve that feels wonderful and matches all your current goals and values? Make a list of things that feel great and are a rewarding treat for yourself so next time you've got a whole lot of ideas of ways to treat yourself to something new that you also deserve.
Done.

Following this pattern of questioning will soon get you into that powerful *cause* place where you can take new actions and generate a new result. In cases where your why is about something more life changing than muffin habits, the process is still the same. Without choosing to question yourself, if is possible for your important relationships to come to a grinding halt as an effect of things that have been occurring in the past. Vitality comes to a standstill as an effect of things that have been occurring in the past, too. Your unconscious mind has so much wisdom that you can tap into with the simple power of the right question. You just need to choose to ask.

"There is no why. Nothing more will I teach you today."—Yoda

Have you ever done this kind of thing to yourself? I don't want to ask: "Why didn't it work out?" so how can I make sure that it definitely works out . . . let me make sure everything is totally perfect before I begin.

When a client tells me, "I'm a perfectionist," I always like to enquire as to their definition of 'perfect'. By holding tight to the idea that everything has to be perfectly correct, we often don't take the action that's required. Sometimes we take no actions at all, out of fear that it may not be perfect—in our own eyes, to our own standards or within the standards of others. But here's the thing: if you never take the action, you'll never know and you'll never be in a position to learn anything new. Heck our own evolution as a planet of life forms has come from reproductive action and genetic 'mistakes' that turned out to be better than what was planned (If you subscribe to Darwin's theory of evolution). I think a significant proportion of our race's greatest discoveries may have come from accidents that weren't in the original plan. There was a great blog posted by David Pegg on May 14, 2012, called "25 Accidental Inventions that Changed the World." *http://list25.com/25-accidental-inventions-that-changed-the-world* and the discoveries include things like plastic and the first implantable pace maker.

What if these people weren't taking any action out of fear that it might not be perfect?

What if your new definition of perfect could be this: I have a vision, I make a plan, I take action, with awareness I see the results of that action, I make changes where required and take *new* actions based on the feedback I receive. Rinse and repeat if necessary.

A perfect student is one who is willing to take action, receive feedback and take new action based on that feedback. In that way, we continue to learn and progress. We may grow 'up' and leave school but hopefully, we never stop learning and growing as human beings.

Where would you be now if that first attempt to do wees in the big toilet was your last because it didn't go perfectly the first time you tried?

Human beings learn through the process of trial and correction. This is how we gather knowledge and end up book-smart, life-smart, and emotionally smart. If action is the missing ingredient for you then I heartily suggest that you either answer the why question and then make the changes you need to or stop being afraid of having to ask yourself the why question after the fact and just take actions toward your goals. Both will lead you to the much more enjoyable wise place.

"I've missed more than 9000 shots in my career. I've lost almost 300 games. 26 times, I've been trusted to take the game winning shot and missed. I've failed over and over and over again in my life. And that is why I succeed." Michael Jordan

Today's Commitment to Authentic Personal Power

Today's commitment is to do something, *anything* that moves you towards achieving one of your goals. Make sure it's simple and easy to do and doesn't require a whole host of specific conditions that are outside of your control.

Here's an example: You've been talking about getting a new car, but need to sell the one you have. Post an advertisement today.

Another example would be to choose one of those sticky life situations that have been calling you into the whys and run yourself through the questions:

How can I do it differently in the future?

And/or

How can I make changes right now that will change things?

DAY 39

The myth of going backwards

We are all works in progress and that's perfect

You cannot de-evolve just as an oak tree doesn't grow smaller with each passing year. I see a lot of clients who have this idea that there was some previous point in their lives when everything was just hunky-dory and if they could just get back to feeling like that 'old' self, all would be well. I disagree. I also see a lot of people who've invested in self-development and who've experienced the life-changing results only to think that they're doing something wrong when life presents another challenge.

I have fallen apart many times over the years, but I've also learned how to put myself together many times as a result. Now when that stuff happens, I just skip the long and drawn out falling apart process and put myself back together in record time. I allow the feelings to be there, learning what I need to learn and move onward and upwards.

When you have a tragedy occur, or just a series of crappy experiences in a row, it DOES NOT MEAN that you've gone backwards. This just means you're still alive and life is a mixed bag of experiences that we learn and grow within. Even enlightened beings lose loved ones and feel that loss in the physical dimension. The most successful of us all can still experience sickness or make a business decision that doesn't result in higher profit.

The most annoying thing in the personal development industry, in my opinion, is all the courses and products that are sold as the answer to everything, as if life is this thing you can master with one tool. Buy the tools and read the books, but know it doesn't end with the right 'thing' or 'tool' because you will continue to evolve. The only single answer is knowing that 'You' are the answer. No one and no 'thing' can give you what you're not looking for, or open to receiving.

I continue to invest in myself, in healing and self-development. This isn't because I'm dissatisfied, but because I want to continue to feel the joy of life, to grow, learn, do more and be more.

The clients who I've mentioned in this book, who've experienced life-changing transformation still stay in touch with me. They understand that they will continue to learn and grow and want to grow into that with support because each new level of newness is still *new*.

It's actually much more like this picture. As we learn and grow and expand, we may revisit the same life situations for a number of reasons. Perhaps we didn't learn what we needed to the first time, or we needed to see things from a new perspective. Or have the opportunity to put our learning into practice. For example, if you are new to expressing yourself, you may attract in many opportunities to practice. Remember, we learn everything though trial and correction, right? So, if someone crosses your boundaries or violates your trust then you will respond differently depending on how many cycles you've done in your evolutionary, upwards spiral. If you really look at your history and the journey towards your 'now,' you may start to see you have made changes and tried new things—that's growth.

I used to think that if I got angry that meant I had low vibration and was therefore doing something 'wrong' in my commitment to personal growth. Now, like I described in Day 7, I know that intense reactions are goal posts for my next step. I am put in new situations and therefore experience new responses. One of my favorite sayings is: "We are all works in progress." We are . . . and that's perfect. Adding to your life experiences brings you another step away from where you were and that means one step closer to where you want to be. How exciting is it that you now have some tools to use for every swing around the cycle of life? You can choose what to focus on and what to invest in. What will happen if, from now on, you give yourself total permission to be a work in progress? What would it be like if you knew *that* was perfect? There will always be something to work on and improve, if you choose to. It is normal to change, grow, and want more for yourself and your life—this is evolution and it only goes forward.

I love the analogy of astronauts when they fly to the moon—they are off course over 90% of the time and it is those little corrections back to the chosen path that makes the destination something they are going to arrive at, or not.

In your life, you have arrived at so many destinations. Think of all the milestones and experiences you've looked forward to and are now a part of the rich tapestry of your life experiences thus far. So often what we strive to achieve, a few years on can be a drudgery. You were born to reach your moon and then set your sights on another. You can be totally at peace in and of yourself and still be working your way towards the next moon on your path of choice.

With each level of evolution, as your knowledge and vibration increases, you have increased capacity to see more possibilities for yourself . . . isn't that wonderful?

You're not, and have never been, going backwards . . . so it's onwards we go!

"Always going forwards, because we can't find reverse, star trekking across the Universe," Star Trekin' lyrics.

Today's Commitment to Authentic Personal Power

Reflect on the questions below and write down your thoughts. Think of how you used to be mentally, emotionally, physically and energetically in contrast to your resources now.

1) Looking backwards over your life, can you see the forward movement? Even if you just had another relationship end, put some weight on or experienced another conflict at work, can you see how you are more than you were before?

2) What's changed?

3) What's the same that you still want to work with?

4) Knowing that you've grown in the last five years, how will these 'same old' situations actually be new and different now?

5) What new perceptions are you now capable of and what might your new response be?

DAY 40

Changing You = Changing the World Part 2

The role you can play in making your community, country, and planet an uplifted and harmonious place to be

In Changing You = Changing the World Part 1, we looked at your immediate circumstances and close relationships. You now know, and have already experimented with changes you can make to open up your relationships. Since then, we've talked about the frequency of thoughts and emotions. We've acknowledged that sometimes certain people can be draining or uplifting to be around (including you). And following that, we've looked at all kinds of ways you can lift your vibration to shift into feeling better, healthier, and more positive. What I want to look at today is how that shift in turn affects the people around you.

What would your day be like if everyone you interacted with was completely at *cause* and taking actions from their inspiration? When you asked: "How are you?" They would answer in an uplifting way, yes? Have you considered that you can be one of those people? You can be the person who leaves a trail of uplifted people in your wake as you move through the day. If you are in a *blurky* place and have to put a lot of energy into pretending that you're happy and positive (when you're not) it will be exhausting, and you'll feel let down if your results don't match your intention (and worse if people aren't very grateful for your efforts). When you choose to do this uplift-everyone-in-your-path thing and are in a high vibrational state, it is easy and effortless—kind of like someone with a huge back-yard lemon tree. They have bags of lemons to give away and don't care who takes them. If you'd spent a year cultivating a single lemon, you'd consider it a rare and precious gift and the receiver should be very, very grateful or you may feel hurt and unappreciated. With lemons coming out the wazoo, so many they're just going to go to waste on the ground, you would be a lot less invested in the outcome of your sharing. The same is true for your vibration—when it's high it is just super easy to be kind, patient, generous, and fun to be around. So, being at *cause* and creating an uplifting vibration, so you feel good doesn't just benefit you, it creates a ripple effect that benefits every person you interact with from your close loved ones to the shop keepers you get your groceries from (and everyone else in the store, too).

There is something else that happens when people start spending more time at *cause* that has a much wider, impactful reach. They start to understand the power of each individual to instigate and support social and global changes. They stop regularly looking out at the state of the world and thinking: "What can one individual do?" They start more often asking themselves: "How can I begin or contribute to the changes I yearn for?" Mahatma Gandhi taught us, "You must be the change you wish to see in the world." I am not suggesting that every empowered individual needs to dedicate their lives to the kinds of dramatic changes that have you still being revered 60+ years after your death. What I am suggesting is that empowered individuals begin to see the changes they can instigate or contribute to on a daily basis in their interactions with other people and each and every time they choose to spend money. As consumers demand more social responsibility from huge corporations, corporations must respond to consumer pressure or lose our business (and therefore their business). Here are some examples:

- An ever-expanding percentage of retailers across the world are stocking organic products in direct response to consumer demands. This is creating better health and vitality for human beings animals and the land itself.
- There is a not-for-profit organization called Choose Cruelty Free (http://www. choosecrueltyfree.org.au/) and any companies that want to use the logo must sign a legally binding agreement about their ingredients and research and manufacturing processes. Huge companies have gone through their accreditation process so that they can display that logo and be purchased by consumers who don't want to buy products that came into being through animal torture.
- There are now societal pressures driving organisations to be environmentally responsible. If you go to your local store, you will see that there is a real demand for environmentally friendly products. This social and environmental point of difference is something consumers value enough to pay more. Go and look in the toilet paper section of the grocery store and see how many companies have put the effort in to having sourced at least some of their materials from sustainable farming or recycled paper. Now think about how much toilet paper is used throughout the world each day—your choices actually do save trees.

The Fair Trade Association also has a logo that some consumers are looking to see on their produce because they want to make sure that they are supporting trade justice and fair working conditions. From producer through to consumer this logo represents that the product has a positive impact on our lives, the lives of others, and the environment.

There are many ways that you can contribute to the incredible transformations that are occurring on our planet right now. By supporting the businesses you respect you are putting money into the economy that supports many causes that change our world for the better.

Rick Slash said, "No single drop of water thinks it's responsible for the flood." I think of this as I exercise consumer choice. We are all part of the flood of change that is occurring due to increased demands from empowered choosers.

Now, consider this for a moment:

- There is no actual separation between us as people and the rest of the universe as we're all mostly energy, just of different densities, and therefore, part of the universal whole.

And

- Thoughts and feelings all have a vibration and are being sent out and received by us all as energetic information.

So, bearing these concepts in mind, does it make sense then that all frequencies are available to everyone?

Just as it makes sense that we are all contributing to and drawing from the totality of vibrations available?

Just like each individual consumer impacts global buying trends, I believe that each individual contributes to the frequencies that exist and are most prevalent at any given moment.

Imagine the cone below represents a Universal Dial, like a radio of frequencies that starts down the bottom with a very slow-moving, dense energy and moves up into fast-moving, clear and light energy. Let's imagine that low, slow, *blurky* energy sits in the constricted bottom of the cone, and that in the middle is contentment. In the expanded energy above are the frequencies of peace, love, gratitude and inspiration. From the middle on upwards you are more able to see the beauty in yourself, other people, and in the world. You are better able to appreciate the absolute magnificience and significance that is Beautiful You.

Now visualise the difference between spending time with a genuinely miserable person and a genuinely happy and inspired person. Does it makes sense that a significant percentage of the world's population being at *cause* and taking inspired action would be a different world to be in? Does it makes sense that a significant percentage of the world's population being at effect, feeling disempowered and hopeless would energetically create a very heavy, slow and hard place to be? It makes sense to me that the more people contributing their energy to the upper eshalons of this cone, the easier it is for those below to tap into that vibration too as it's more prevalent.

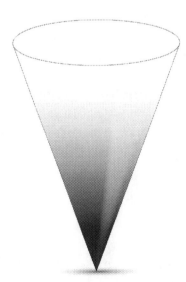

I like to think of it this way: The first time someone walks through tall grass, there is no path to follow. The more the path is walked, the easier it is to see. The more people that follow that exact path, the clearer, and easier it becomes to follow and even see from a distance. Likewise, some of the first spiritual teachers and expanded thinkers had a hard time and were met with a whole lot of, often deadly, resistance to their vision of expansion. Now, so many have walked that path that our text books reflect those expanded ideas about the science of life and countless teachers across the world are safely teaching people that they are powerful and their futures are in their own hands.

So many of the world's atrocities occur because of low-vibration, blame and fear. These feelings are driving the need to overpower and 'win' over others, just like bullies in a playground of children. No one who genuinely loves themselves needs to dominate others in order to be powerful.

What do you think it would it be like to live in a community populated by human beings awakened to their innate resources and taking responsibility for their own happiness? What would it be like if everyone knew they were in charge of their lives? What would it be like if most partnerships were between happy adults that functioned as a team to be more than the sum of their separate parts? What would change? What would stay the same? I think blame would be eradicated. If everybody felt secure and confidant in themselves as an energetic, powerful being then there would be no need to control another person just to feel powerful. If people felt secure, there would be no need to make sure you had a gun in the house or be afraid if your neighbour has a different belief system than you.

Have you ever been to an event with hundreds of people and felt the excitement build as the event was about to start? This is an energetic experience of a group focused on a single, exciting thing. Have you ever been a student of meditation or joined an exercise group and found it easier to get into the right zone when you're surrounded by people with the same focus? This, too, is group energy at work. Most people I know can be also be swept upwards into the happiness of someone else's happiness.

Can it makes sense for you that this is happening on a global scale also?

Every individual that's inspired to be the best version of themselves, to love themselves and love life goes out into the world and makes choices that make their relationships, their communities and the planet a better place to be. Even when that commitment is invisible, and only energetic, it is still such a meaningful and accumulatively powerful contribution to the whole.

What do you think?

Would it be possible for you, over each year, to make more energetic deposits into the frequencies of contentment and happiness than those lower, denser vibrations in the bottom of the cone? If that started to be your reality, what would immediately start happening within and all around you? What do you think the long-term effects would be? For yourself? For your family? And for your community? If there were lots of communities being this way across the world . . . What do you think would be possible?

If this matches your current beliefs about energy, or is compelling enough to explore some more, there are all kinds of organisations and groups that meet for the purpose of raising energy. These include things like worldwide meditations where thousands of people meditate at the same time focusing on specific outcomes. I've joined these meditations many times and find them similar to meditating in a large group that is right there in the room with you.

Why not look into something like that and experience it for yourself?

Today's Commitment to Authentic Personal Power

Use one of the many tools you know to raise your energy throughout the day. Take that energy with you and share it in every interaction. Smile and speak kindly to all the people you come across, even if they're not normally the kind of people you'd make conversation with. In times of silence, intentionally feel positive feelings and imagine that you're infusing the air with that positivity and uplifting everyone within a 10 kilometre radius. Notice how it feels to intentionally be out and about sharing positivity, in your manner and just by being 'Beautiful You'.

DAY 41

Self Assessment Day (#2)

*Looking at your unconscious beliefs after 33 more days of
transformation and empowerment from the inside out*

When I meet a client or student for the first time and listen to their hopes and dreams, all I see in my mind's eye is future-them achieving the vision they have for themselves. Sometimes new people come into my clinic that are not yet ready to have a vision other than knowing they need to feel better than they currently do. In all instances, I envision them in that better place. I am always looking for a way to support them to get from their not-as-enjoyable-as-it-could-be 'now' into living the reality they've said they would prefer. I have one of the most rewarding careers I've ever heard of because I have front row seats to one of the best shows on Earth—human beings harnessing their wholistic vitality and authentic personal power. From this empowered place new thoughts, feelings, actions, and sensations create a flow-on effect that noticeably improves areas of their life that were not even on the to-do list. Each and every one of these transformations begins in a single moment with a single shift. As you proceed to this self-assessment day, and discover even one change, please know this means you have begun and will continue to renovate and upgrade your perspectives and programming. Keep a record, if you choose to, of what you write down today and come back to it in twelve months' time. Even if a single word or phrase that has new wording next to it (than what you wrote on Day 8), that means those significant changes have begun. What you write in twelve months' time will be different again. You will continue to learn, grow and change and remember; evolution is always forwards.

Today's Commitment to Authentic Personal Power:

As with the instructions on Days 8 and 9, please read the word or words and write down the very first thing that comes to your mind. If there are multiple meanings or multiple things that immediately blurt up into conscious awareness then make note of it all.

Health _____

_____

Spirituality _____

_____

Personal development _____

_____

Family _____

_____

Money _____

_____

Relationships _____

_____

Feminine power

_____

Masculine power

_____

Career

_____

Community

_____

Love

_____

Intimacy

_____

Sex

_____

Making love

Marriage

Exercise

"I love myself"

Mother

Father

Brother

Sister

Daughter

Son

Husband

Wife

Ex-Partner

Self esteem

Getting what I want

Failure

Wellness

Sickness

Pain

How others see me

What others think of me

Motivation

_____

Procrastination

_____

I am worthy

_____

I am beautiful

_____

I am wanted

_____

I belong

_____

I am loved

_____

I am tolerated

Saying "yes"

I'm unlovable

I'm not good enough

I am amazing

Personal power

Coming first

Manifestation

Debt

Planet Earth

Human beings

My diet

Abundance

We are all created equal

Anger

Sadness

Fear

Hurt

Guilt

I am successful

Saying "no"

Contributing

Being vulnerable

Friends

Honesty

Intelligence

I am clever

I am worthy

I am enough

I am a meaningful part of the whole

Before moving on to our final day in this 42 day journey, I want you to take stock of your answers above and celebrate each and every shift and change.

Also take a moment (or a whole heap of moments) to celebrate yourself for being here, all the way at the almost-end of the book. Can you imagine how many people still have this on their shelves or sitting with a book-mark sticking out somewhere up near the beginning? Or on their reader with a whole lot of other fantastic stuff they've not read yet. But you are here, you've made it, you invested in yourself and if you've just completed the exercise today, then you've put 100% effort into your authentic personal power and you know what that means . . . you're in the process of achieving 100% of the rewarding results.

DAY 42

Conclusion

Hip Hip Hooray . . . onwards and upwards we go!

First things first, please accept my congratulations on your commitment to this ongoing process. You deserve all the wonderful experiences, feelings, relationships and successes that will be the result of your devotion to being authentically powerful 'You'.

Does this mean that you're going to be at your very best, every second of every day? Hell no! What it does mean is that you've hopefully given yourself permission to be a living, breathing work-in-progress. You can be a happy, hopeful, inspired, and inspiring person and you can also experience every other emotion available too. You now know that life's *blurky* moments are part of your ongoing learning and no *blurk* has to be a permanent feature in your life, unless for some reason it is serving you and you want to stay there.

You are in possession of three components: your mind, your body and life-force energy—all are in a constant state of movement and change. With these three components you are able to directly affect and be empowered with your 'now'.

To experience this Authentic Personal Power you needed to:

- Understand how you are and have been creating your life experiences with your mind, body and life-force energy. I hope you have enjoyed learning about your innate resources and how you create your 'now' with them.
- Learn to live at *cause*—Step into the driver's seat of life and know that you're in charge of it.
- Gain a lot of easy-to-use tools for stepping into your power and uplifting the moment— the potent 'now' where all of life's empowerment takes place.

You may have heard before that changing your thoughts is a positive and powerful thing to do but sometimes that's damned near impossible due to the intensity of what you're feeling. I wanted you to have a recipe book of ingredients and a manual for understanding that sometimes those emotions need to be listened to and not distracted away. Sometimes, once you understand them, you need to get out and do something physical before you can relax and change your thoughts. Sometimes you need to shift your energy before your body can follow suit. You now have a tool kit for feeling empowered to create change regardless of what is happening in your 'now'.

It's OK to keep on searching for new techniques, products, people, and places to feel great about. As human beings we are designed to grow and expand just like an oak tree. It's natural to want to deepen our roots and widen our branches. There is a very different energy to searching based on "I'm-not-enough-right-now ness" and searching because you want to keep on growing and learning. The energy of life moves and as happy people we move with it.

It's also OK (in fact it is my heartfelt recommendation) to get support during this process of learning and growth. Every successful person I know has a team of support—professionals in specific areas of expertise lending their wisdom to encourage, maintain, and enhance that success. For some, the team includes various staff and people like financial advisors, accountants, health professionals, IT consultants, house cleaners, child minders and marketing experts. No one creates sustainable success in isolation. I find it baffling how comfortable some people are to see an accountant or website designer but those same people might not want to share their thoughts and feelings with a professional whose area of expertise it is to support them in accessing more enjoyable thoughts and feelings. I am on the support team for all of my clients. I understand their patterns and hold the space for them to transform in their own unique way. You deserve that kind of understanding and support when you want to create changes in your circumstances.

You might feel as though promises broken by other people are the most hurtful experiences of your life, but believe me, no relationship is more important than the one you have with you. I used to have a little note on my fridge from one of those desk-top day calendars with a quote a day. It said, "Every time you settle for the unacceptable, a part of you inside dies." I needed it there as a constant reminder while I was in the process of learning to respect myself and set healthy boundaries. When I work with people who are healing from a damaging relationship they arrive often feeling like they need to heal from what the other person has done. A major part of healing is acknowledging all the times they'd broken promises to themselves. Next time they do x, I'm going to do y. Then they do x and you still don't take the new action. The good thing about knowing this stuff is that you now can take responsibility for how you feel and take new actions to feel better. You are in charge. And your relationship with you is the most important relationship in your life. It is vital that you treat yourself the way you wish to be treated by the outside world. If you want new results, it's time to take new actions. And by investing in yourself you will create miracles.

There's never been a better time than right now for you to acknowledge and celebrate the unique wonder that is beautiful, perfect 'You'!

The last pages of this book are a quick reference guide with lots of ways to uplift your moment. Please know this section is not an advertisement with snappy suggestions for the art of distraction and suppressing your emotions. Your feelings are your greatest guidance system. They let you know what your head is up to, what circumstances are working for you and when things need to change. The questions on Day 16 will assist you to gain clarity about the situation and if the *blurkyness* is still there then this quick guide has lots of options to change your state of being and start moving in a new direction. Sometimes, due to life's other commitments, we need to snazz ourselves up into feeling better even when we are processing emotional events (like we need to go into a customer service job, but are feeling heartbroken over last week's break up)—the list will help you to access the best states possible while you are needing to function at a higher level than you feel like being in.

In every moment of every day you get to choose the kind of person you want to be. Your innate resources are a synchronised team working for 'You'. You are amazing and powerful. You are an energetic being, having a human experience and, as such, you are intricately individual and radiantly alive. Every day you can celebrate your magnificence by stepping into your power and choosing to be in charge of 'You'.

Your future is in your hands and will be determined by the accumulative total of your collective 'now's. You have the tools to shift your perspective, to be at *cause* and empower your life to drive in the direction of your heart's longings. You have all the raw ingredients you need.

You are *The Answer* you've been looking for.

Today's Commitment to Authentic Personal Power

1) Feel satisfied, gratified and proud!
2) Have a read through the "Uplift Your Moment" section that follows today. It's good to be familiar with the ideas and make your own notes, following my list, of the things you know make you feel better. All you need to do then is remember the list when you're feeling blurky.

"Every day's the beginning . . . it's up to me to choose, who I am and where I'm going to,"
Lyrics from Positively Funky track "Love's Alive"

Ways to Uplift Your Moment—Quick Reference Guide

List of quick and easy ways to kick-start
your empowerment in 5 minutes or less

Self-love is making the decision to look at this list.

Empowerment is reading through, finding the one that *erks* you the least, and actually doing it.

The purpose of this section is for you to have a quick list of things to do when you find yourself at effect. If you read through the list and think, "urrrgh! I don't wanna do any of this stuff," then head back to Day 16—and read the "Staying in my *blurk* for what purpose section."

Go on . . . you totally deserve a kick-start to feeling-much-better process and it starts now:

1) Put on one of your favourite songs of all time, one that, if it comes on the radio you make everyone else there be quiet and just LOVE it and don't tire of listening to it.
   —It must be song that has only positive associations
   —If you're in a position to be able to get up and dance or move your body (even if it's a car-bop) do that, too
   —If you're not in a situation where you can get your hands on the song, just sing it out loud or inside your head.

2) BREATHE—take 10 breaths with focused conscious attention. Breathe in through your nose as deeply and slowly as possible and FILL your lungs with air, hold for a moment and then slowly breathe it out.

3) Run as fast as you can until you run out of breath, then with long, slow deep recovery breaths, walk back to home/work or wherever you started (this is a FANTASTIC way to release frustration!)

4) Meditation, just for even five minutes will shift your energy. Five minutes every day will change your life for the better.

5) Call the most positive friend or colleague that you know. Get distracted and then uplifted by their awesomeness.

6) Put on a track/clip/movie that makes you laugh every time and then . . . laugh.

7) Take your mind back to a time in the past when you've laughed so hard and so long that your face hurt. Close your eyes and imagine travelling back to that exact moment, channel back into your body and relive the moment, imagine reliving it again, see what you saw, hear what you heard, make it a big, colourful picture inside your mind. If that's hard, just imagine telling someone else about it (and even laugh now at how the other person just doesn't get how bloody hilarious it was because they weren't there).

8) What's a movie you've watched and laughed in—right now, think of the funniest scene . . .

9) If you've ever learned the salute to the sun in yoga then do that, right now.
—Give yourself permission to get it wrong and focus only on celebrating your choice to improve your 'now'.

10) Tickle yourself (just kidding).

11) Make a list of 55 things/experiences/moments that you are grateful for.

12) Hug someone.

13) Hold yourself and say the words: "(Your name)   , everything is going to be alright," over and over. If you can do that for a couple of minutes, then ask your librarian (your unconscious mind)—what else can I do to improve my now?

14) If you've ever learned some qi gong, take a few minutes to do the movements you remember—it will get things moving.
—Give yourself permission to get it wrong and focus only on celebrating your choice to improve your 'now'.

15) Go outside and get some sunshine on your skin.

16) Go for a five minute walk.

17) Think of the last great time you had . . . really use your powerful mind, body, and energy for the power of positivity and remember the fun you had.

18) If you have some young children nearby—play a quick game with them (they really know how to have fun and be in the moment and laugh with their whole beings).

19) Have a cup of your favourite tea.

20) Take five minutes to visualise one of your most exciting goals being realised.

21) Take five minutes to daydream something fantastic (complete escapism with no 'reality' required).

22) Give yourself a pep talk in the same way that you would pump up a good friend.

23) Walk barefoot on the grass or sand.

24) Take some flower essences specific to your needs.

25) Clean for five minutes—scrub the toilet, do the dishes, tidy up some paperwork . . . and feel great about it.

26) Change the sheets on your bed—then tonight you'll be able to lie down in crisp cleanliness . . . yay!

27) Take a few minutes for the pranayama (alternate nostril breathing) from Day 27—The Power of Breath Part 2.

28) Make a plan to catch up with someone you adore.
(If you don't have someone in your life that you adore then this suggestion transforms into: Make a plan to meet someone you adore. There are lots of ways to meet new people— make a plan to try one out).

29) Listen to my affirmation song, "All the Lights are Green,"—it's free when you download my e-book so you don't even need to spend any money to feel better now. This song is a boppy affirmation that will guide your unconscious mind into realising that the

pathways to happiness are clear (and if you're stopped at a 'red light' then it's just a message that there's something to do, not a message about your worthiness).

30) Massage your hands and feet—it will get things moving and feel lovely, too.

31) Stand in front of a mirror with the broadest and most enthusiastic, fake smile you can muster. Hold that, looking yourself in the eye, until you can laugh (at yourself or the process) and enjoy the actual smile that eventuates.

32) Suggest to someone else to try number 31 (it will make you both smile).

33) Give yourself permission to be at effect. Get a pen and paper and blurt out all the *blurk*! This kind of cathartic release often clears the fog and allows clarity to over.

34) Hug your pet (or if your pet is something un-huggable, like a fish, then maybe have a heart to heart chat with him or her instead).

35) Plunge your head into a barrel of cold water or have someone slap you in the face (well . . . it always seems to work in the movies!)

36) Fill all your plugs of conscious awareness with a bunch of other (more fun) stuff.

37) Get cracking on setting some new goals—redirect that limitless mind of yours on to creating some satisfying newness. If you want help you can access my free resource, "How to set goals you'll achieve," e-book at *www.wholisticvitality.com.au*

38) Make an appointment to see a wise and inspiring friend or the therapist of your choice.
Allow yourself to be supported with whatever is going on. No one heals in isolation—we all prosper mentally, physically and energetically with internal and external assistance.

39) Shout out, "There can be only One," and stalk confidently into your next encounter.

40) Get started on an orgasm.

41) Take silly pictures with a friend. Make faces, laugh . . . just have fun. Then when you are having a bad day, you can go back and laugh at these pictures. I would recommend taking them on your phone so they are always with you.

42) Ask yourself: What's one thing that I can do right now to move me in the direction of one of my short-term goals? And go and take that immediate action. You'll feel better immediately.

The last one is go to *www.wholisticvitality.com.au* and download my "Recommendations for Ongoing Authentic Personal Power" if you feel like new ideas for more long-term solutions.

Recommended List for Further Reading

The personal development industry is alive with new talent, ideas and inspiration. As such, I keep an up-to-date recommended reading list on my website. This allows me to add new resources to it as I come across them. This is a completely free resource—you don't need to put in an email address or any other personal information.

Just go to *www.wholisticvitality.com.au* and click on the Recommended Reading List for continuing your journey of Authentic Personal Power.

A personal note from the author

As I said in the introduction, I wrote this book with a heartfelt passion to support people in connecting with the power of their innate resources. As such, I would absolutely love to hear from you with your stories and experiences of reading The Answer. Your emails are welcomed at theanswer@wholisticvitality.com.au